糸東流空手形全集

第四巻

THE COMPLETE SERIES OF SHITO-RYU KATA

VOL.4

ワンシュー	WANSYU
松村セーサン	MATSUMURA SESAN
心　波	SHINPA
アーナンコウ	ANANKO
サイファ	SAIFA
クルルンファ	KURURUNFA

監修　全日本空手道連盟糸東会

SUPERVISION:JAPAN KARATEDO FEDERATION SHITO-KAI

糸東流の理念

　糸東流空手道の流祖・摩文仁賢和は、首里手の大家・糸洲安恒先生のもとで糸洲派の空手道を、また那覇手の大家・東恩納寛量先生より東恩納派を学んだ。さらに松村派、新垣派などの各派も修めた後に、糸洲派と東恩納派の流れを「摩文仁流」と提唱。"守破離"の段階を経て精査・精選し、その精髄を融合させた。そして、糸洲・東恩納両先生の頭文字を取り「糸東流」と称したのである。

　形を根幹とし、内容を現実的かつ理論的に究明。その結果を分解組手に応用して練習することが、糸東流空手の最大の特徴である。そして無駄な力を使わず、必要以上に大きな動作も行わない。従って、形も派手な動作はないが、その反面、技の内容が理解しやすいので、生きた形を演武することができる。

　また、流祖は技術指導のみならず精神教育にも重点を置き『君子之拳』を標榜して、円満な人格者の養成にも尽力された。

　糸東流は分派が多いが、糸東会は、糸東流の本流を結集し、さらなる普及発展に努力を続ける。

Philosophy of Shito-ryu

Shito-ryu karate-do was founded by Kenwa Mabuni who dedicatedly learned karate-do under Ankoh Itosu Sensei, a grand master of Shuri-te first and later Kanryo Higaonna Sensei, a grand master of Naha-te and also other masters of several schools and systems such as Matsumura-ha and Aragaki-ha. Kenwa Mabuni learned both strains of Itosu and Higaonna and named the mixed of two as "Mabuni-ryu" and after going through the stage of "Shu-Ha-Ri", or the stage where he surpassed his mentors in terms of techniques, mentality and strength, and he carefully selected and extracted a main techniques from the mixture, he integrated this extracted main techniques. And he named his school Shito-ryu by taking one Kanji character each from the grand masters' name, Itosu and Higaonna Sensei.

Study kata realistically and theoretically. And apply the result to the "Bunkai-kumite" and practice it. This is the most important characteristic of Shito-ryu-karate.Also as another characteristic, it doesn't have any large movement more than necessary due to avoidance of using unnecessary power but we can perform Kata lively due to the good comprehension of Kata.

Also, the founder put an importance on the philosophical education, He advocated "Kunshi no Ken" or "Karate-do for men of integrity" and educated disciples for improving and nururing a harmonious character. Shito-ryu has many systems but Shito-Kai unifies these systems and strives for diffusing and developing Shito-ryu Karate.

はじめに

　糸東流の空手道は流祖摩文仁賢和から伝承された多くの形を継承している。我々はその形を正しく学び、そして後世に伝えていく責務がある。糸東流は形を根幹としその技術、精神を学ぶところに真髄がある。
　また形にはその技の意味を伝える分解組手があるが、単に形を演武することに留まらず、分解組み手を習熟することにより活きた形とすることができるのである。
　本書では分解組み手の基本的な解釈を一指針として示しているが、これをもとに更に深い研究がなされることを期待している。
また、新しい試みとして足型に運足の進行を点線で示した。本書が皆様の空手道のさらなる研鑽に役立つことを願うものである。

全日本空手道連盟糸東会
会長　岩田源三

Introduction

Shito-ryu Karate-do has inherited many Kata that have been passed down by Kenwa Mabuni, the founder of Shito-ryu. We have a responsibility to learn these Kata correctly and teach them to future generations. The essence of Shito-ryu is to treat the Kata as the basis while learning their techniques and spirit.
Kata have Bunkai Kumite that express the meaning of each technique. By mastering Bunkai Kumite instead of simply demonstrating Kata, it is possible to make the Kata more livelier.
This book presents basic interpretations of Bunkai Kumite as guiding principles, but I hope that it serves as a foundation for more in-depth research.
In addition, as a new endeavor, I indicated the progression of foot maneuvers for Kata with dotted lines. I wish that this book serves of use in your studies of Karate-do.

Japan Karatedo Federation Shito-kai
President Genzo Iwata

目次
contents

糸東流の理念 ·· 002

Philosophy of Shito-ryu ······························· 003

はじめに　Introduction ······························· 004

ワンシュー　WANSYU ····························· 006

松村セーサン　MATSUMURA SESAN ········ 024

心　波　SHINPA ···································· 056

アーナンコウ　ANANKO ······················ 076

サイファ　SAIFA ·································· 100

クルルンファ　KURURUNFA ··············· 126

監修者・演武者紹介 About the Supervisors & the Performers ··········· 156

ワンシュー

　ワンシューは、 糸洲系首里手の形で比較的短い形であるが、 前半部には猫足立ち
の下段払い、 手刀受けの技が多く、 更に交差立ちへの寄り足、 上段打ちから突き
への変化など、 この形独特な要素が含まれる。
　猫足立ちの安定、 そして機敏な動きが求められる。

Wansyu is a Shuri-te Kata of Itosu's system. Although it is a relatively
short Kata, it includes some distinctive components. The first half uses
Shuto-uke and Gedan Barai in the Nekoashidachi stance extensively,
and it also includes such things as entering the Kosadachi stance
through Yori-ashi and transitioning from a Jodan Uchi to a Tsuki (punch.)
It demands stability of the Nekoashidachi stance and quick movements.

WANSYU

ワンシュー　形の流れ

気を付けの姿勢	礼	直立	用意	1 挙動	2 挙動
 ①	 ②	 ③	 ④	 ⑤	 ⑥

8 挙動	9 挙動	10 挙動	11 挙動	12 挙動	13 挙動
 ⑬	 ⑭	 ⑮	 ⑯	 ⑰	 ⑱

20 挙動	21 挙動	22 挙動	23 挙動	24 挙動	25 挙動
 ㉕	 ㉖	 ㉗	 ㉘	 ㉙	㉚

気を付けの姿勢	礼	気を付けの姿勢
 ㊲	 ㊳	㊴

ワンシュー

3 挙動 / 4 挙動 / 5 挙動 / 6 挙動 / 7 挙動 / 途中動作

14 挙動 / 15 挙動 / 16 挙動 / 17 挙動 / 18 挙動 / 19 挙動

26 挙動 / 27 挙動 / 28 挙動 / 29 挙動 / 30 挙動 / 止め

気を付けの姿勢	礼	直立

❶	❷	❸
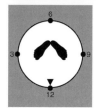		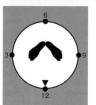

立ち方／結び立ち。 手の動作／両手を伸ばし、大腿部外側に付ける。	立ち方／結び立ち。	立ち方／結び立ち。 手の動作／両手を伸ばし、大腿部外側に付ける。
Stance: Musubidachi. Hands: Stretch both arms with hands putting on both sides of the thighs.	Stance: Musubidachi.	Stance: Musubidachi. Hands: Stretch both arms with hands putting on both sides of the thighs.

● 挙動の分解　Kumite in detail

用意	1 挙動	2 挙動

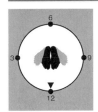

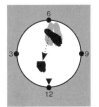

足の動作／踵を軸に上足底を内側に寄せる。
立ち方／閉足立ち。
手の動作／両拳を下腹部前に構える。

Feet: Bring the upper sole to the inside with the heel as the axis.
Stance: Heisokudachi.
Hands: Put both fists in front of the lower abdomen.

足の動作／そのまま。
立ち方／閉足立ち。
手の動作／水月の前に右拳上、左拳下に拳一つ分あけて構える。

Feet: Keep in the same position as ❹.
Stance: Heisokudachi.
Hands: Leave one fist and hold the right fist up and the left fist down in front of the solar plexus.

足の動作／右足を12時方向へ運ぶ。
立ち方／右猫足立ち。
手の動作／右下段払い。左拳は脇に引く。

Feet: Bring the right foot in the direction of 12 o'clock.
Stance: Right Nekoashidachi.
Hands: Do Right Gedan Barai. Pull the left fist to armpit.

ワンシュー

011

3 挙動	4 挙動	5 挙動

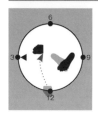		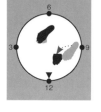

足の動作／右足を3時方向へ運ぶ。
立ち方／右猫足立ち。
手の動作／右下段払い。左拳は脇に引く。

Feet: Bring the right foot in the direction of 3 o'clock.
Stance: Right Nekoashidachi.
Hands: Do Right Gedan Barai. Pull the left fist to armpit.

足の動作／そのまま。
立ち方／右猫足立ち。
手の動作／左中段逆突き。右拳は脇に引く。

Feet: Keep in the same position as ❼.
Stance: Right Nekoashidachi.
Hands: Do Left Chudan Gyaku-zuki. Pull the right fist to armpit.

足の動作／左足を12時方向へ運ぶ。
立ち方／左猫足立ち。
手の動作／左下段払い。右拳は脇に引く。

Feet: Bring the left foot in the direction of 12 o'clock.
Stance: Left Nekoashidachi.
Hands: Do Left Gedan Barai. Pull the right fist to armpit.

●挙動の分解　Kumite in detail

2挙動〜4挙動

右中段突きを左斜め後方に転身して猫足立ちとなり右下段払い受け。

Block the Right Chudan Zuki by shifting your body back to the left, and performing a Right Gedan-barai-uke in the Nekoashidachi stance.

左中段逆突きで極める。

Finish with a Left Chudan Gyaku-zuki.

6 挙動　　　　　7 挙動　　　　　途中動作

 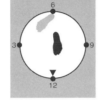 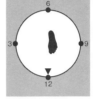

足の動作／そのまま。
立ち方／左猫足立ち。
手の動作／左中段手刀受け。右拳はそのまま。

Feet: Keep in the same position as ❾.
Stance: Left Nekoashidachi.
Hands: Do Left Chudan Shuto-uke. Right fist as it is.

足の動作／右足を上げる。（左膝内側に添える。）
手の動作／右上段裏打ち。左手は右肘に添える。

Feet: Raise the right leg.(attach to the inside of the left knee)
Hands: Do Right Jodan Ura-uchi. The left hand attaches to the right elbow.

足の動作／そのまま。
手の動作／右拳を左腕下より回す。

Feet: Keep in the same position as ⓫.
Hands: Pass the right fist under the left arm.

5挙動〜9動

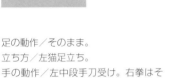   

相手の右中段蹴りを、右後方に転身して、左下段払い受け。

Block your opponent's Right Chudan Geri by shifting your body back to the right and performing a Left Gedan-barai-uke.

続いて相手の右中段突きを左手刀受け。

Next, block your opponent's Right Chudan Zuki with a Left Shuto-uke.

すかさず上段裏打ちをする。相手の上段揚げ受けで捌かれたところ。

Immediately perform a Jodan Ura-uchi. At this point, your opponent blocks with a Jodan Age-uke.

相手の上段揚げ受けをくぐるように右中段突きを行う。

Pass under your opponent's Jodan Age-uke with a Right Chudan Zuki.

8 挙動	9 挙動	10 挙動

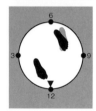	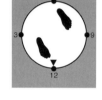	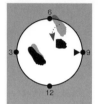

足の動作／右足を 12 時方向へ運ぶ。
立ち方／右半前屈立ち。
手の動作／右中段順突き。左拳は脇に引く。

Feet: Bring the right foot in the direction of 12 o'clock.
Stance: Right Han-zenkutudachi.
Hands: Do Right Chudan Jun-zuki. Pull the left fist to armpit.

足の動作／そのまま。
立ち方／右半前屈立ち。
手の動作／左中段逆突き。右拳は脇に引く。

Feet: Keep in the same position as ⑬.
Stance: Right Han-zenkutudachi.
Hands: Do Left Chudan Gyaku-zuki. Pull the right fist to armpit.

足の動作／左足を 9 時方向へ運ぶ。
立ち方／左猫足立ち。
手の動作／左下段払い。右拳は脇に引く。

Feet: Bring the left foot in the direction of 9 o'clock.
Stance: Left Nekoashidachi.
Hands: Do Left Gedan Barai. Pull the right fist to armpit.

●挙動の分解　Kumite in detail

更に左中段逆突きで極める。

Finish with a Left Chudan Gyaku-zuki.

11 挙動	12 挙動	13 挙動

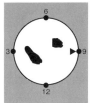	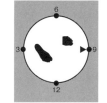	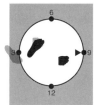

ワンシュー

足の動作／そのまま。
立ち方／左猫足立ち。
手の動作／左中段手刀受け。右拳はそのまま。

Feet: Keep in the same position as ⑮.
Stance: Left Nekoashidachi.
Hands: Do Left Chudan Shuto-uke. Right fist as it is.

足の動作／そのまま。
立ち方／左猫足立ち。
手の動作／右中段逆突き。左拳は脇に引く。

Feet: Keep in the same position as ⑮.
Stance: Left Nekoashidachi.
Hands: Do Right Chudan Gyaku-zuki. Pull the left fist to armpit.

足の動作／右足を9時方向へ運ぶ。
立ち方／右猫足立ち。
手の動作／右中段手刀受け。左拳はそのまま。

Feet: Bring the right foot in the direction of 9 o'clock.
Stance: Right Nekoashidachi.
Hands: Do Right Chudan Shuto-uke. Left fist as it is.

10挙動〜12挙動

相手の中段突きを右後方に転身して猫足立ちになり左中段払い受け。

Block your opponent's Chudan Zuki by shifting your body back to the right and performing a Chudan Harai-uke in the Nekoashidachi stance.

更に相手の中段逆突きを手刀受けで捌く。

Block your opponent's Chudan Gyaku-zuki with a Shuto-uke.

右中段逆突きで極める。

Finish with a Right Chudan Gyaku-zuki.

14 挙動　　　15 挙動　　　16 挙動

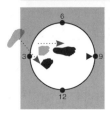

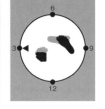

足の動作／右足を踏み出し更に左足を引き付ける（寄り足）。
立ち方／交差立ち。
手の動作／左中段突き。右拳は脇へ引く。

Feet: Step on the right foot, then attract the left foot.(Yoriashi)
Stance: Kosadachi.
Hands: Do Left Chudan Zuki. Pull the right fist to armpit.

足の動作／そのまま。
立ち方／交差立ち。
手の動作／右下段払い。左拳は甲を下にし、水月前に引く。

Feet: Keep in the same position as ⑲.
Stance: Kosadachi.
Hands: Do Right Gedan Barai. Make the back of the left fist face down and pull it in front of the solar plexus.

足の動作／左足を3時方向へ運び、反時計回りで3時方向を向く。
立ち方／左猫足立ち。
手の動作／左下段払い。右拳は脇へ引く。

Feet: Bring the left foot in the direction of 3 o'clock and turn counterclockwise same direction.
Stance: Left Nekoashidachi.
Hands: Do Left Gedan Barai. Pull the right fist to armpit.

●挙動の分解　Kumite in detail

相手の左中段突きを右手刀受け。
Block your opponent's Left Chudan Zuki with a Right Shuto-uke.

相手の手を取り左中段逆突きで極める。
Take your opponent's hand and finish with a Left Chudan Gyaku-zuki.

突きを捕られる。
Your punch is caught.

相手の掴んだ手を水月に引き寄せる。
Pull your seized hand by opponent towards your solar plexus (Suigetsu).

17 挙動　　18 挙動　　19 挙動

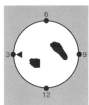 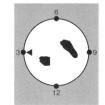 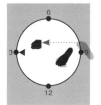

足の動作／そのまま。
立ち方／左猫足立ち。
手の動作／左中段手刀受け。右拳はそのまま。

Feet: Keep in the same position as ㉑.
Stance: Left Nekoashidachi.
Hands: Do Left Chudan Syuto-uke. Right fist as it is.

足の動作／そのまま。
立ち方／左猫足立ち。
手の動作／右中段逆突き。左拳は脇へ引く。

Feet: Keep in the same position as ㉑.
Stance: Left Nekoashidachi.
Hands: Do Right Chudan Gyaku-zuki. Pull the left fist to armpit.

足の動作／右足を3時方向へ運ぶ。
立ち方／右猫足立ち。
手の動作／右中段手刀受け。左拳はそのまま。

Feet: Bring the right foot in the direction of 3 o'clock.
Stance: Right Nekoashidachi.
Hands: Do Right Chudan Shuto-uke. Left fist as it is.

(反対側から見たところ)

(the view from the other side)

右下段払いではずす。

Release the arm with a Right Gedan Barai.

(反対側から見たところ)

(the view from the other side)

左上段逆突きで極める。

Finish with a Left Jodan Gyaku-zuki.

20 挙動　　21 挙動　　22 挙動

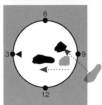 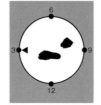 

足の動作／右足を踏み出し、更に左足を引き付ける（寄り足）。
立ち方／交差立ち。
手の動作／左中段突き。右拳は脇へ引く。

Feet: Step on the right foot, then attract the left foot.(Yoriashi)
Stance: Kosadachi.
Hands: Do Left Chudan Zuki. Pull the right fist to armpit.

足の動作／そのまま。
立ち方／交差立ち。
手の動作／右下段払い。左拳は甲を下にし、水月前に引く。

Feet: Keep in the same position as ㉕.
Stance: Kosadachi.
Hands: Do Right Gedan Barai. Make the back of the left fist face down and pull it in front of the solar plexus.

足の動作／左足を12時方向へ運ぶ。
立ち方／左基立ち。
手の動作／左下段払い。右拳は脇へ引く。

Feet: Bring the left foot in the direction of 12 o'clock.
Stance: Left Motodachi.
Hands: Do Left Gedan Barai. Pull the right fist to armpit.

●挙動の分解　Kumite in detail

相手の右中段突きを右斜め後方に転身し、左中段払い受け。

Block your opponent's Right Chudan Zuki by shifting your body back to the right, and performing a Chudan Harai-uke.

更に左中段突きを右中段流し受け。

Block the Left Chudan Zuki with a Right Chudan Nagashi-uke.

左中段突きで極める。

Finish with a Left Chudan Zuki.

23 挙動　　24 挙動　　25 挙動

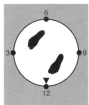

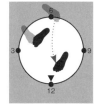

足の動作／そのまま。
立ち方／左基立ち。
手の動作／右掌底にて中段流し受け。
左拳は脇へ引く。

Feet: Keep in the same position as ㉗.
Stance: Left Motodachi.
Hands: Do Chudan Nagashi-uke with Right Shote. Pull the left fist to armpit.

足の動作／右足を12時方向へ運ぶ。
立ち方／右基立ち。
手の動作／右中段横受け。左下段払い。

Feet: Bring the right foot in the direction of 12 o'clock.
Stance: Right Motodachi.
Hands: Do Right Chudan Yoko-uke and Left Gedan Barai

足の動作／左足を12時方向へ運ぶ。
立ち方／左基立ち。
手の動作／左中段横受け。右下段払い。

Feet: Bring the left foot in the direction of 12 o'clock.
Stance: Left Motodachi.
Hands: Do Left Chudan Yoko-uke and Right Gedan Barai.

24挙動～28挙動

相手の右中段突きを右斜め後方に転身し、左中段払い受け。

Block your opponent's Right Chudan Zuki by shifting your body back to the right, and performing a Left Chudan Harai-uke.

左中段突きを右足を後方に引き前屈立ちとなり、右中段横受けで捌く。

Block the Left Chudan Zuki by drawing your right leg back and performing a Right Chudan Yoko-uke in the Zenkutsudachi stance.

左中段蹴りを左足を左に移し、後屈立ちでかわし下段払い。

Dodge the Left Chudan Geri by moving your left leg to the left and performing a Gedan Barai in the Kokutsudachi stance.

右上段突きを前屈立ちとなり、右上段揚げ受け。

Block the Right Jodan Zuki by performing a Right Jodan Age-uke in the Zenkutsudachi stance.

019

26 挙動

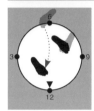

足の動作／右足を12時方向へ運ぶ。
立ち方／右基立ち。
手の動作／右中段横受け。左下段払い。

Feet: Bring the right foot in the direction of 12 o'clock.
Stance: Right Motodachi.
Hands: Do Right Chudan Yoko-uke and Left Gedan Barai.

27 挙動

足の動作／左足を後方へ運ぶ。
立ち方／後屈立ち。
手の動作／右下段払い。左拳は甲を下に向けて水月前に構える。

Feet: Bring the left foot to the back.
Stance: Left Kokutsudachi.
Hands: Do Right Gedan Barai. Make the back of the left fist face down and pull it in front of the solar plexus.

28 挙動

足の動作／左足を動かし、6時方向へ向く。
立ち方／左前屈立ち。
手の動作／左上段揚げ受け。右拳は脇へ引く。

Feet: Bring the left foot to the left and turn the body in the direction of 6 o'clock.
Stance: Left Zenkutsudachi.
Hands: Do Left Jodan Age-uke. Pull the right fist to armpit.

●挙動の分解　Kumite in detail

左中段逆突きで極める。

Finish with a Left Chudan Gyaku-zuki.

29 挙動　　　　30 挙動　　　　止め

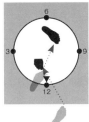
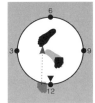
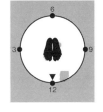

足の動作／右足を6時方向へ運び、更に左足を6時方向へ運ぶ。(反時計回り)
立ち方／右猫足立ち。
手の動作／右中段手刀受け。左手は水月前に構える。

Feet: Bring the right foot in the direction of 6 o'clock, and bring the left foot in the direction of 6 o'clock. (Counterclockwise)
Stance: Right Nekoashidachi.
Hands: Do Right Chudan Shuto-uke. Hold the left hand in front of the solar plexus.

足の動作／右足を6時方向へ引く。
立ち方／左猫足立ち。
手の動作／左中段手刀受け。右手は水月前に構える。

Feet: Bring the right foot in the direction of 6 o'clock.
Stance: Left Nekoashidachi.
Hands: Do Left Chudan Shuto-uke. Hold the right hand in front of the solar plexus.

足の動作／左足を引き寄せる。
立ち方／閉足立ち。
手の動作／両拳を下腹部前に構える。

Feet: Pull the left foot to right foot.
Stance: Heisokudachi.
Hands: Hold the both fists in front of the lower abdomen

---

29 挙動

相手の右中段突きを左後方に転身し、猫足立ちとなり右手刀受け。
相手の手を取り右中段前蹴り。
更に中段逆突きで極める。

Block your opponent's Right Chudan Zuki by shifting your body back to the left and performing a Shuto-uke in the Nekoashidachi stance.
Take your opponent's hand and perform a Right Chudan Mae-geri.
Finish with a Chudan Gyaku-zuki.

気を付けの姿勢	礼	気を付けの姿勢
 ㊲	 ㊳	 ㊴

足の動作／そのまま。
立ち方／結び立ち。
手の動作／両開手を大腿部外側へ付ける。

Feet: Keep in the same position as ㊱.
Stance: Musubidachi.
Hands: Stretch both arms with hands putting on both sides of the thighs.

●挙動の分解　Kumite in detail

ワンシュー

松村セーサン

　松村セーサンは、 立ち方にセーサン立ちという特殊な立ち方があり、 バラ手、 歩み足(忍び足)からの蹴り足、 刺股受け等、 独特な技が見られる。
　前半は基本動作が続き呼吸と身体の締めを意識しての動作であるが、 後半は蹴り技からの突き、 より足からの受け等変化に富んだ動きの早い形である。

Matsumura Sesan features the distinctive "Sesandachi" stance, as well as various unique techniques, such as Bara-te, Keri-ashi from Ayumi-ashi (Shinobi-ashi), and Sasumata-uke.
The first half consists of basic movements involving awareness of breathing and body tension, but the second half of this fast Kata includes a rich variety of movements, including Tsuki (punches) transitioning from Keri (kicks) and blocks transitioning from Yori-ashi.

MATSUMURA SESAN

気を付けの姿勢	礼	直立	用意	1挙動	2挙動
 ①	 ②	 ③	 ④	 ⑤	 ⑥

9挙動	途中動作	途中動作	10挙動	11挙動	12挙動
 ⑬	 ⑭	 ⑮	 ⑯	 ⑰	 ⑱

19挙動	20挙動	21挙動	22挙動	23挙動	24挙動
 ㉕	 ㉖	 ㉗	 ㉘	 ㉙	 ㉚

31挙動	32挙動	33挙動	34挙動	移行動作	裏打ちしたところ
 ㊲	 ㊳	 ㊴	 ㊵	 ㊶	 ㊷

松村セーサン

3 挙動
⑦

4 挙動
⑧

5 挙動
⑨

6 挙動
⑩

7 挙動
⑪

8 挙動
⑫

13 挙動
⑲

14 挙動
⑳

15 挙動
㉑

16 挙動
㉒

17 挙動
㉓

18 挙動
㉔

25 挙動
㉛

26 挙動
㉜

27 挙動
㉝

28 挙動
㉞

29 挙動
㉟

30 挙動
㊱

35 挙動
㊸

移行動作
㊹

移行動作
㊺

36 挙動
㊻

37 挙動
㊼

38 挙動
㊽

39 挙動	移行動作	移行動作	40 挙動	移行動作	移行動作

㊾	㊿	51	52	53	54

45 挙動	46 挙動	47 挙動	48 挙動	49 挙動	50 挙動

61	62	63	64	65	66

気を付けの姿勢	礼	気を付けの姿勢

73	74	75

41 挙動	42 挙動	43 挙動	44 挙動	移行動作	裏打ちしたところ
 ㊺	 ㊻	 ㊼	 ㊽	 ㊾	 ㊿

51 挙動	途中動作	52 挙動	53 挙動	止め	止め
 ㊼	 ㊽	 ㊾	 ㊿	 ㋀	 ㋁

松村セーサン

気を付けの姿勢	礼	直立

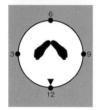	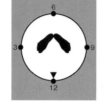	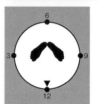
立ち方／結び立ち。 手の動作／両手を伸ばし、大腿部外側に付ける。 Stance: Musubidachi. Hands: Stretch both arms with hands putting on both sides of the thighs.	立ち方／結び立ち。 Stance: Musubidachi.	立ち方／結び立ち。 手の動作／両手を伸ばし、大腿部外側に付ける。 Stance: Musubidachi. Hands: Stretch both arms with hands putting on both sides of the thighs.

●セーサン立ち／Sesandachi

【足の位置】
後ろ足の爪先と前足の踵との間隔は後ろ足の膝を折り曲げた長さで、この時の前足の踵と後ろ足の親指の先は横一直線上から一足長前足を前に出した位置にある。
(三戦立ちから前足を一足長前に出した位置)
前足の爪先の横方向の線と後ろ足の踵の横方向の線と、前足足刀部の縦方向の線と後ろ足足刀部の縦方向の線は正方形となる。

【爪先の方向】
前足は正面に対し約30度(内側)。
後ろ足は足刀部が正面を向く。

【膝の曲げ方】
足の裏を床面に密着させ膝をやや内側に曲げる様にして臀部を上方に引き締める。
膝は爪先方向にやや曲げ、腰を落として下半身を締める。

【重心】
両足間の中央。上体を正面に向ける。

【Position of the feet】
With the tip of the toes of the back foot and the heel of the front foot far enough apart that the knee of the back leg is bent, the feet are positioned with the front foot one step ahead from the point where the heel of the front foot and the tip of the big toe of the back foot would be aligned along a horizontal line. (The front foot is one step ahead from its position in Sanchin-dachi.)
A square is formed by the horizontal line extending from the tip of the toes of the front leg and the horizontal line extending from the heel of the back foot, together with the vertical line extending from the Sokuto part of the front foot and vertical line extending from the Sokuto part of the back foot.

【Direction of the toes】
The front foot is turned approximately 30 degrees inward from the front. The Sokuto part of the back foot faces frontward.

【Bending of the knees】
Fix the bottom of your feet firmly against the surface of the floor, bend the knees slightly inward, and tighten the upper part of the buttocks. Bend the knee slightly in alignment with the toes, with the waist lowered and the lower half of the body kept tense.

【Center of gravity】
The center between both legs. Face the upper body forward.

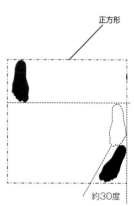

用意	1 挙動	2 挙動

足の動作／右足を3時方向へ運ぶ。
立ち方／外八字立ち。
手の動作／両手を握り下腹部前に構える。

Feet: Bring the right foot in the direction of 3 o'clock.
Stance: Sotohachijidachi.
Hands: Put both fists in front of the lower abdomen.

足の動作／左足を12時方向へゆっくり円を描くように運ぶ。
立ち方／左セーサン立ち。
手の動作／左中段横受け。右拳は脇に引く。

Feet: Bring the left foot so that it draws a circle from the inside slowly in the direction of 12 o'clock.
Stance: Left Sesandachi.
Hands: Do Left Chudan Yoko-uke. Pull the right fist to armpit.

足の動作／そのまま。
立ち方／左セーサン立ち。
手の動作／右中段逆突き。左拳は脇に引く。

Feet: Keep in the same position as ❺.
Stance: Left Sesandachi.
Hands: Do Right Chudan Gyaku-zuki. Pull the left fist to armpit.

●挙動の分解　Kumite in detail

相手の左中段追い突きに対し、右斜め後方へ転身し、左中段横受け。

Block your opponent's Left Chudan Oi-zuki by shifting your body back to the right, and performing a Left Chudan Yoko-uke.

右中段突きで反撃。

Counter with a Right Chudan Zuki.

さらに相手が右中段突きを出すので、右中段横受け。

Your opponent strikes again with a Right Chudan Zuki, so perform a Right Chudan Yoko-uke.

3 挙動

4 挙動

5 挙動

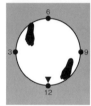  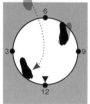 

足の動作／そのまま。
立ち方／左セーサン立ち。
手の動作／右中段横受け（素早く）。左拳は脇に引く。

Feet: Keep in the same position as ❺.
Stance: Left Sesandachi.
Hands: Do Right Chudan Yoko-uke (quickly). Pull the left fist to armpit.

足の動作／右足を 12 時方向へゆっくり円を描くように運ぶ。
立ち方／右セーサン立ち。
手の動作／そのまま。

Feet: Bring the right foot so that it draws a circle from the inside slowly in the direction of 12 o'clock.
Stance: Right Sesandachi.
Hands: Keep in the same position as ❼.

足の動作／そのまま。
立ち方／右セーサン立ち。
手の動作／左中段逆突き。右拳は脇に引く。

Feet: Keep in the same position as ❽.
Stance: Right Sesandachi.
Hands: Do Left Chudan Gyaku-zuki. Pull the right fist to armpit.

●挙動の分解　Kumite in detail

Counter with a Left Chudan Zuki.

032

6 挙動　　　　　7 挙動　　　　　8 挙動

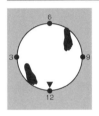
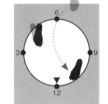
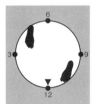

足の動作／そのまま。
立ち方／右セーサン立ち。
手の動作／左中段横受け（素早く）。右拳は脇に引く。

Feet: Keep in the same position as ❽.
Stance: Right Sesandachi.
Hands: Do Left Chudan Yoko-uke (quickly).Pull the right fist to armpit.

足の動作／左足を12時方向へゆっくり円を描くように運ぶ。
立ち方／左セーサン立ち。
手の動作／そのまま。

Feet: Bring the left foot so that it draws a circle from the inside slowly in the direction of 12 o'clock.
Stance: Left Sesandachi.
Hands: Keep in the same position as ❿.

足の動作／そのまま。
立ち方／左セーサン立ち。
手の動作／右中段逆突き。左拳は脇に引く。

Feet: Keep in the same position as ⓫.
Stance: Left Sesandachi.
Hands: Do Right Chudan Gyaku-zuki. Pull the left fist to armpit.

9 挙動　　　　　途中動作　　　　　途中動作

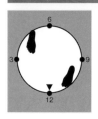

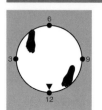

足の動作／そのまま。
立ち方／左セーサン立ち。
手の動作／右中段横受け（素早く）。左拳は脇に引く。

Feet: Keep in the same position as ⓫.
Stance: Left Sesandachi.
Hands: Do Right Chudan Yoko-uke (quickly). Pull the left fist to armpit.

Transition Movement　　　　Transition Movement

●挙動の分解　Kumite in detail

10 挙動

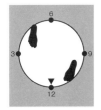

足の動作／そのまま。
立ち方／左セーサン立ち。
手の動作／人差し指一本拳で挟み突き。
（拳、肘は水平に胸の高さ）

Feet:Keep in the same position as ⑪.
Stance: Left Sesandachi.
Hands: Do Hasami-zuki by both Ipponken with index finger.(elbows and fists level at chest height)

11 挙動

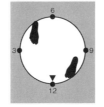

足の動作／そのまま。
立ち方／左セーサン立ち。
手の動作／人差し指一本拳（甲が上）で中段双手突き（雁下）。

Feet: Keep in the same position as ⑪.
Stance: Left Sesandachi.
Hands: Do Chudan Morote-zuki (to Ganka) by both Ipponken (hands back up).

12 挙動

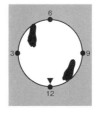

足の動作／そのまま。
立ち方／左セーサン立ち。
手の動作／両手をバラ手で上段へ打ち込む。（開手にて胸前から前面に円を描くように）

Feet:Keep in the same position as ⑪.
Stance: Left Sesandachi.
Hands: Strike the Jodan with both Barate.(as draw a circle forward from the chest front by open both hands)

相手が肩を掴もうとしてくる瞬間。
Your opponent is about to grab your shoulders.

人差し指一本拳で相手の脇腹を突く。
Strike your opponent's sides with an index finger Ippon ken.

さらに雁下を人差し指一本拳で突く。
Strike the Ganka (rib cage below the nipples) with an index finger Ippon ken.

バラ手で目潰しを行う。
Strike at your opponent's eyes with a Bara-te.

035

13 挙動　　14 挙動　　15 挙動

⑲

⑳

㉑

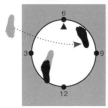  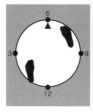  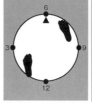 

足の動作／左足を軸に右足を9時方向へ運ぶ。（右回りで身体と目付けは6時方向）
立ち方／右セーサン立ち。
手の動作／両開手で下方へ掌底にて押さえる。（体側から拳一つぐらい空ける）

Feet: Bring the right foot in the direction of 9 o'clock pivoting on the left foot.(Do it in a clockwise direction. The line of sight and body are in the direction of 6 o'clock)
Stance: Right Sesandachi.
Hands: Push downward by the Shotei of both open hands.(spacing one fist from both sides)

足の動作／そのまま。
立ち方／右セーサン立ち。
手の動作／両開手を前面で交差しながら右開手中段横受け。左掌底にて下方へ押さえる。

Feet:Keep in the same position as ⑲.
Stance: Right Sesandachi.
Hands: After crossing the open hands at the front, do Chudan Yoko-uke by right open hand and the left Shotei presses the lower part.

足の動作／そのまま。
立ち方／右セーサン立ち。
手の動作／右掛手。左開手はそのまま。

Feet:Keep in the same position as ⑲.
Stance: Right Sesandachi.
Hands: Do Right Kakete.The left open hand is the same position as ⑳.

●挙動の分解　Kumite in detail

背後から掴まれようとした時

掌底にて急所を攻撃。

Your opponent is about to seize you from behind.

Strike your opponent's crotch with your Shotei.

036

16 挙動　　　17 挙動　　　18 挙動

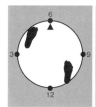

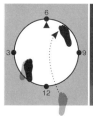

足の動作／左足を6時方向へゆっくり円を描くように運ぶ。
立ち方／左セーサン立ち。
手の動作／両開手を前面で交差しながら左開手中段横受け。右掌底にて下方へ押さえる。

Feet: Bring the left foot so that it draws a circle from the inside slowly in the direction of 6 o'clock.
Stance: Left Sesandachi.
Hands: Cross the open hands at the front. Do Left Kaisyu Chudan Yoko-uke and the right Shotei presses the lower part.

足の動作／そのまま。
立ち方／左セーサン立ち。
手の動作／左掛手。右開手はそのまま。

Feet:Keep in the same position as ㉒.
Stance: Left Sesandachi.
Hands: Do Left Kakete. The right open hand is the same position as ㉒.

足の動作／右足を6時方向へゆっくり円を描くように運ぶ。
立ち方／右セーサン立ち。
手の動作／両開手を前面で交差しながら右開手中段横受け。左掌底にて下方へ押さえる。

Feet: Bring the right foot so that it draws a circle from the inside slowly in the direction of 6 o'clock.
Stance: Right Sesandachi.
Hands:Cross the open hands at the front. Do Right Kaisyu Chudan Yoko-uke and the left Shotei presses the lower part.

14挙動〜19挙動

相手の右中段突きを左斜め後方へ転身して、右中段横受けを行う。

Block your opponent's Right Chudan Zuki by shifting your body backwards to the left, and performing a Right Chudan Yoko-uke.

横受けした突きを素早く取る。

Quickly seize the arm that you blocked.

体の向きを変え、掌底で攻撃。

Change the direction of your body and strike with your Shotei.

19 挙動	20 挙動	21 挙動

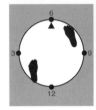  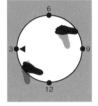 

足の動作／そのまま。
立ち方／右セーサン立ち。
手の動作／右掛手。左開手はそのまま。

Feet: Keep in the same position as ㉔.
Stance: Right Sesandachi.
Hands: Right Kakete. Left Kaishu as it is.

足の動作／足の位置をそのままで上足底を中心に左回りで3時方向を向く。
立ち方／左セーサン立ち。
手の動作／左中段横受け。右拳は脇へ引く。
＊20挙動〜24挙動連続動作

Feet: Turn the body counterclockwise in the direction of 3 o'clock pivoting on the upper soles.
Stance: Left Sesandachi.
Hands: Do Left Chudan Yoko-uke. Pull the right fist to armpit.
＊20 to 24 movements are continuous.

足の動作／そのまま。
立ち方／左セーサン立ち。
手の動作／右中段逆突き。左拳は脇へ引く。

Feet: Keep in the same position as ㉖.
Stance: Left Sesandachi.
Hands: Do Right Chudan Gyaku-zuki. Pull the left fist to armpit.

●挙動の分解　Kumite in detail

相手の右中段突きを右斜め後方へ転身して、左中段横受けを行う。

Block your opponent's Right Chudan Zuki by shifting your body back to the right, and performing a Left Chudan Yoko-uke.

相手の中段突きに対して、突き受けを行う。

Block your opponent's Chudan Zuki with a Tsuki-uke.

左中段順突きで攻撃。

Strike with a Left Chudan Jun-zuki.

右中段前蹴り。

Right Chudan Mae-geri.

038

22 挙動

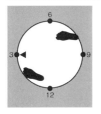

足の動作／そのまま。
立ち方／左セーサン立ち。
手の動作／左中段順突き。右拳は脇へ引く。

Feet: Keep in the same position as ㉗.
Stance: Left Sesandachi.
Hands: Do Left Chudan Jun-zuki. Pull the right fist to armpit.

23 挙動

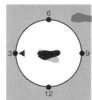

足の動作／右中段前蹴り。
手の動作／そのまま。

Feet: Do Right Chudan Mae-geri.
Hands: Keep in the same position as ㉘.

24 挙動

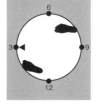

足の動作／蹴った右足を9時方向へ素早く引く。
立ち方／左セーサン立ち。
手の動作／右中段逆突き。左拳は脇へ引く。

Feet: Pull the right foot quickly in the direction of 9 o'clock.
Stance: Left Sesandachi.
Hands: Do Right Chudan Gyaku-zuki. Pull the left fist to armpit.

松村セーサン

右中段逆突き。
Right Chudan Gyaku-zuki.

25 挙動　　　　26 挙動　　　　27 挙動

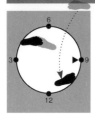
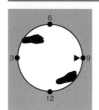
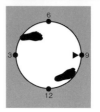

足の動作／左足を軸にして右足を12時方向へ右回りで運ぶ。
立ち方／右セーサン立ち。
手の動作／右中段横受け。左拳は脇へ引く。
＊25挙動〜29挙動連続動作

Feet: Bring the right foot clockwise in the direction of 12 o'clock pivoting on the left foot.
Stance: Right Seisandachi.
Hands: Do Right Chudan Yoko-uke. Pull the left fist to armpit.
＊25 to 29 movements are continuous.

足の動作／そのまま。
立ち方／右セーサン立ち。
手の動作／左中段逆突き。右拳は脇へ引く。

Feet:Keep in the same position as ㉛.
Stance: Right Sesandachi.
Hands: Do Left Chudan Gyaku-zuki. Pull the right fist to armpit.

足の動作／そのまま。
立ち方／右セーサン立ち。
手の動作／右中段順突き。左拳は脇へ引く。

Feet:Keep in the same position as ㉛.
Stance: Right Sesandachi.
Hands: Do Right Chudan Jun-zuki. Pull the left fist to armpit.

●挙動の分解　Kumite in detail

28 挙動

29 挙動

30 挙動

足の動作／左中段前蹴り。
手の動作／そのまま。

Feet: Do Left Chudan Mae-geri.
Hands: Keep in the same position as ㉝.

足の動作／蹴った左足を3時方向へ素早く引く。
立ち方／右セーサン立ち。
手の動作／左中段逆突き。右拳は脇へ引く。

Feet: Pull the left foot quickly in the direction of 3 o'clock.
Stance: Right Sesandachi.
Hands: Do Left Chudan Gyaku-zuki. Pull the right fist to armpit.

足の動作／足の位置をそのまま上足底を中心に左回りで6時方向を向く。
立ち方／左セーサン立ち。
手の動作／左中段横受け。右拳は脇へ引く。
＊30挙動〜34挙動連続動作

Feet: Turn the body counterclockwise in the direction of 6 o'clock pivoting on the upper soles.
Stance: Left Sesandachi.
Hands: Do Left Chudan Yoko-uke. Pull the right fist to armpit.
＊ 30 to 34 movements are continuous.

31 挙動

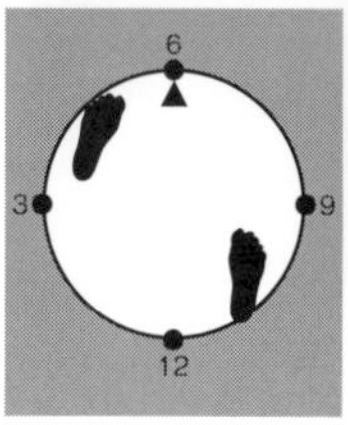

足の動作／そのまま。
立ち方／左セーサン立ち。
手の動作／右中段逆突き。左拳は脇へ引く。

Feet: Keep in the same position as ㊱ .
Stance: Left Sesandachi.
Hands: Do Right Chudan Gyaku-zuki. Pull the left fist to armpit.

32 挙動

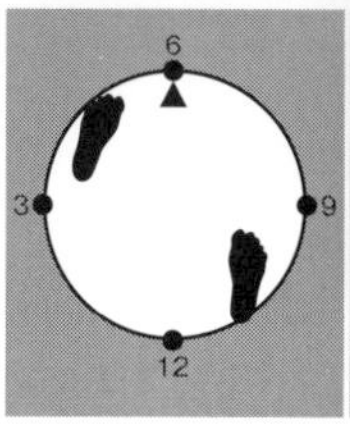

足の動作／そのまま。
立ち方／左セーサン立ち。
手の動作／左中段順突き。右拳は脇へ引く。

Feet: Keep in the same position as ㊱ .
Stance: Left Sesandachi.
Hands: Do Left Chudan Jun-zuki.Pull the right fist to armpit.

33 挙動

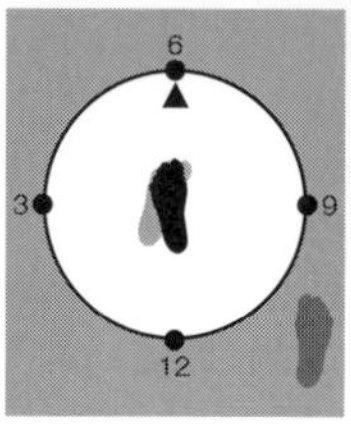

足の動作／右中段前蹴り。
手の動作／そのまま。

Feet: Do Right Chudan Mae-geri.
Hands: Keep in the same position as ㊳ .

●挙動の分解　Kumite in detail

34 挙動 　　　移行動作　　　裏打ちしたところ

足の動作／蹴った右足を12時方向へ素早く引く。
立ち方／左セーサン立ち。
手の動作／右中段逆突き。左拳は脇へ引く。

Feet: Pull the right foot quickly in the direction of 12 o'cloke.
Stance: Left Sesandachi.
Hands: Do Right Chudan Gyaku-zuki. Pull the left fist to armpit.

Transition Movement

Transition Movement (Urauchi)

松村セーサン

35 挙動	移行動作	移行動作

㊸	㊹	㊺

足の動作／左足を軸にして右足を右回りで12時方向へ運ぶ。
立ち方／右猫足立ち。
手の動作／右拳を頭上から上段裏打ち。
＊35挙動〜39挙動連続動作

Feet: Bring the right foot clockwise in the direction of 12 o'clock pivoting on the left foot.
Stance: Right Nekoashidachi.
Hands: Right fist from overhead to do Jodan Ura-uchi.
＊35 to 39 movements are continuous.

足の動作／右足のかかとをつける。
手の動作／そのまま。

Feet: Lower the heel of the right foot.
Hands: Keep in the same position as ㊸.

足の動作／左足を右足前に運ぶ。
手の動作／そのまま。

Feet: Bring the left foot ahead of the right foot.
Hands: Keep in the same position as ㊸.

●挙動の分解　Kumite in detail

相手が後ろから襟を取りに来る。
Your opponent grabs your collar from behind.

即座に振り向いて猫足立ちになりながら上段裏打ちを行う。
Immediately turn around and assume the Nekoashidachi stance while performing a Jodan Ura-uchi.

さらに前足で中段前蹴りを行う。
Perform a Chudan Mae-geri with the front foot.

相手の左中段突きに対し猫足立ち下段払いをを行う。
Block your opponent's Left Chudan Zuki with a Gedan Barai in the Nekoashidachi stance.

36 挙動　　　　　　　　37 挙動　　　　　　　　38 挙動

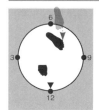

足の動作／右中段前蹴り。
手の動作／そのまま。

Feet: Do Right Chudan Mae-geri.
Hands: Keep in the same position as ㊸.

足の動作／蹴った右足を着地すると同時に寄り足。
立ち方／右猫足立ち。
手の動作／右下段払い。左拳は脇へ引く。

Feet: Slide forward by Yoriashi as soon as put down right foot.
Stance: Right Nekoashidachi.
Hands: Do Right Gedan Barai.Pull the left fist to armpit.

足の動作／そのまま。
立ち方／右猫足立ち。
手の動作／左中段逆突き。右拳は脇へ引く。

Feet:Keep in the same position as ㊼.
Stance: Right Nekoashidachi
Hands: Do Left Chudan Gyaku-zuki. Pull the right fist to armpit.

左中段逆突きで極める。
Finish with a Left Chudan Gyaku-zuki.

39 挙動　　移行動作　　移行動作

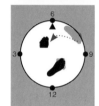
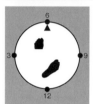

足の動作／右足から猫足のまま寄り足。
立ち方／右猫足立ち。
手の動作／右上段揚げ受け。左拳は脇へ引く。

Feet: Slide forward by right Yoriashi Keeping Nekoashidachi stance.
Stance: Right Nekoashidachi.
Hands: Do Right Jodan Age-uke. Pull the left fist to armpit.

Transition Movement

Transition Movement

●挙動の分解　Kumite in detail

40挙動   移行動作   移行動作

        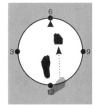

足の動作／右足を軸にして左足を左回りで6時方向へ運ぶ。
立ち方／左猫足立ち。
手の動作／左拳を頭上から上段裏打ち。
＊41～44挙動連続動作。

Feet: Bring the left foot counterclockwise in the direction of 6 o'clock pivoting on the right foot.
Stance: Left Nekoashidachi.
Hands: Left fist from overhead to do Jodan Ura-uchi.
＊ 41 to 44 movements are continuous.

足の動作／左足の踵をつける。
手の動作／そのまま。

Feet: Lower the heel of the left foot.
Hands: Keep in the same position as ㊾.

足の動作／右足を左足前に運ぶ。
手の動作／そのまま。

Feet: Bring the right foot ahead of the left foot.
Hands: Keep in the same position as ㊾.

41 挙動　　　　42 挙動　　　　43 挙動

足の動作／左中段前蹴り。
手の動作／そのまま。

Feet: Do Left Chudan Mae-geri.
Hands: Keep in the same position as ㊾.

足の動作／蹴った左足を着地すると同時に寄り足。
立ち方／左猫足立ち。
手の動作／左下段払い。右拳は脇へ引く。

Feet: Do Yoriashi as soon as landing the kicked left foot.
Stance: Left Nekoashidachi.
Hands: Do Left Gedan Barai. Pull the right fist to armpit.

足の動作／そのまま。
立ち方／左猫足立ち。
手の動作／右中段逆突き。左拳は脇へ引く。

Feet: Keep in the same position as ㊾.
Stance: Left Nekoashidachi.
Hands: Do Right Chudan Gyaku-zuki. Pull the left fist to armpit.

●挙動の分解　Kumite in detail

44 挙動　　　　移行動作　　　　裏打ちしたところ

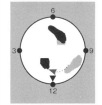

足の動作／左足から猫足のまま寄り足。
立ち方／左猫足立ち。
手の動作／左上段揚げ受け。右拳は脇へ引く。

Feet: Slide forward by left Yoriashi, keeping Nekoashidachi stance.
Stance: Left Nekoashidachi.
Hands: Do Left Jodan Age-uke. Pull the right fist to armpit.

Transition Movement

Transition Movement (Urauchi)

松村セーサン

049

45 挙動

46 挙動

47 挙動

足の動作／左足を軸にして右足を右回りで12時方向へ運ぶ。
立ち方／右猫足立ち。
手の動作／右拳を頭上から上段裏打ち。
＊45挙動〜47挙動連続動作

Feet: Bring the right foot clockwise in the direction of 12 o'clock pivoting on the left foot.
Stance: Right Nekoashidachi.
Hands: Do Jodan Ura-uchi by the right fist from overhead.
＊ 45 to 47 movements are continuous.

足の動作／そのまま。
立ち方／右猫足立ち。
手の動作／左中段逆突き。右拳は脇へ引く。

Feet:Keep in the same position as ㊿.
Stance: Right Nekoashidachi.
Hands: Do Left Chudan Gyaku-zuki.
Pull the right fist to armpit.

足の動作／右足から猫足のまま寄り足。
立ち方／右猫足立ち。
手の動作／右上段揚げ受け。左拳は脇へ引く。

Feet: Slide forward by right Yoriashi, keeping Nekoashidachi stance.
Stance: Right Nekoashidachi.
Hands: Do Right Jodan Age-uke. Pull the left fist to armpit.

●挙動の分解　Kumite in detail

相手の上段追い突きに対し、引き足で猫足立ちになり、上段揚げ受けを行う。

Block your opponent's Jodan Oi-zuki by assuming a Nekoashidachi stance with Hiki-ashi and performing a Jodan Age-uke.

相手の寄り足の右中段逆突きに対し、引き足で猫足立ちになり、手刀受け。

Block your opponent's Yori-ashi Right Chudan Gyaku-zuki by assuming a Nekoashidachi stance with Hiki-ashi and performing a Shuto-uke.

中段前蹴り。

Chudan Mae-geri.

48 挙動　　　　49 挙動　　　　50 挙動

 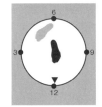 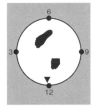

松村セーサン

足の動作／右足を6時方向へ引く。
立ち方／左猫足立ち。
手の動作／左手刀受け。右拳は脇へ引く。

Feet: Pull the right foot in the direction of 6 o'clock.
Stance: Left Nekoashidachi.
Hands: Do Left Shuto-uke. Pull the right fist to armpit.

足の動作／右足にて回し蹴りをするようにして右足底を左掌に当てる。
手の動作／そのまま。
＊49挙動〜51挙動連続動作

Feet: Do like Mawashi-geri with right foot, and hit the left palm with the sole.
Hands: Keep in the same position as ⓺⓸.
＊ 49 to 51 movements are continuous.

足の動作／右足を6時方向へ引く。
立ち方／左猫足立ち。
手の動作／右中段逆突き。左拳は脇へ引く。

Feet: Pull the right foot in the direction of 6 o'clock.
Stance: Left Nekoashidachi.
Hands: Do Right Chudan Gyaku-zuki. Pull the left fist to armpit.

右中段逆突きで極める。

Finish with a Right Chudan Gyaku-zuki.

051

51 挙動	途中動作	52 挙動

足の動作／そのまま。
立ち方／左猫足立ち。
手の動作／左上段揚げ受け。右拳は脇へ引く。

Feet:Keep in the same position as ❻.
Stance: Left Nekoashidachi.
Hands: Do Left Jodan Age-Uke.Pull the right fist to armpit.

足の動作／そのまま。
立ち方／左猫足立ち。
手の動作／左拳を外側に半円を描きながら左脇に引くと同時には開手となる。（掌を前方に向け指先は下向き）

Feet: Keep in the same position as ❻.
Stance: Left Nekoashidachi.
Hands: Draw a semicircle on the outside with a left fist and pull it to the left side, both hands open at the same time.(The palm forward and fingertips pointing downward)

足の動作／そのまま。
立ち方／左猫足立ち。
手の動作／右拳も開手。掌を前方に向け、指先は下向きに構える。

Feet: Keep in the same position as ❻.
Stance: Left Nekoashidachi.
Hands: The right fist also opens. Hold the palm forward and fingertips pointing downward.

●挙動の分解　Kumite in detail

相手の右上段追い突きに対し、引き足で猫足立ちになり、上段揚げ受けを行う。

Block your opponent's Right Jodan Oi-zuki by assuming the Nekoashidachi stance with Hiki-ashi and performing a Jodan Age-uke.

相手の中段前蹴りに対し、刺股受けを行う。

Block your opponent's Chudan Mae-geri with a Sasumata-uke.

上段掌底当てで極める。

Finish with a Jodan Shotei-ate.

53 挙動 　　　　　　　止め　　　　　　　　止め

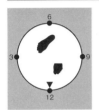
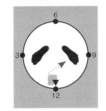

足の動作／そのまま。
立ち方／左猫足立ち。
手の動作／両手の掌底部を合わせて前方下段に押し出す。（刺股受け）

Feet: Keep in the same position as ⓪.
Stance: Left Nekoashidachi.
Hands: Combine the palm bottom of both hands and push it out to the lower front. （Sasumata-uke）

足の動作／左足を右足の横に移動する。
立ち方／外八時立ち。
手の動作／両手を握り下腹部に構える。

Feet: Bring the left foot aside the right foot.
Stance: Sotohatijidachi.
Hands: Hold both hands into a fist and settle on the lower abdomen.

足の動作／右足を左足の横に寄せる。
立ち方／結び立ち。
手の動作／両開手を重ね、下腹部に構える。

Feet: Pull the right foot to the left foot.
Stance: Musubidachi.
Hands: Open both hands and hold them in front of the lower abdomen with the left hand putting on the right hand.

松村セーサン

気を付けの姿勢	礼	気を付けの姿勢

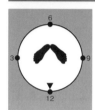	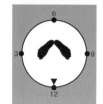	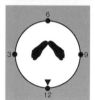

足の動作／そのまま。
立ち方／結び立ち。
手の動作／両開手を大腿部外側へ付ける。

Feet: Keep in the same position as ⑫.
Stance: Musubidachi.
Hands: Stretch both arms with hands putting on both sides of the thighs.

足の動作／そのまま。
立ち方／結び立ち。
手の動作／そのまま。

Feet: Keep in the same position as ⑫.
Stance: Musubidachi.
Hands: Keep in the same position as ⑬.

足の動作／そのまま。
立ち方／結び立ち。
手の動作／そのまま。

Feet: Keep in the same position as ⑫.
Stance: Musubidachi.
Hands: Keep in the same position as ⑬.

● 挙動の分解　Kumite in detail

松村セーサン

心波は、上地流の流れをくむ形である。
繰り受けが特徴の形で、三戦立ちからの動きにリズム感が感じられる。
接近戦からの蹴り技の工夫が必要となる。

Shinpa is a Kata that draws from the Uechi school.
It is a Kata distinguished by its Kuri-uke. A sense of rhythm can be felt in the movements from its Sanchin-dachi stance.
It requires ingenuity in close combat kicking techniques.

SHINPA

心波　形の流れ

気を付けの姿勢  ①

礼  ②

直立  ③

途中動作  ④

用意  ⑤

用意  ⑥

5挙動  ⑬

6挙動  ⑭

7挙動  ⑮

8挙動  ⑯

9挙動  ⑰

10挙動 ⑱

17挙動  ㉕

18挙動  ㉖

19挙動  ㉗

20挙動  ㉘

21挙動  ㉙

22挙動 ㉚

29挙動  ㊲

30挙動  ㊳

止めへの移行動作  ㊴

止め  ㊵

気を付けの動作  ㊶

礼 ㊷

移動動作	途中動作	1挙動	2挙動	3挙動	4挙動
 ⑦	 ⑧	 ⑨	 ⑩	 ⑪	 ⑫

心波

11挙動	12挙動	13挙動	14挙動	15挙動	16挙動
 ⑲	 ⑳	 ㉑	 ㉒	 ㉓	 ㉔

23挙動	24挙動	25挙動	26挙動	27挙動	28挙動
 ㉛	 ㉜	 ㉝	 ㉞	 ㉟	 ㊱

気を付けの姿勢

 ㊸

気を付けの姿勢	礼	直立
 ❶	 ❷	 ❸
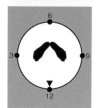		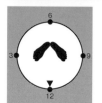

立ち方／結び立ち。
手の動作／両手を伸ばし、大腿部外側に付ける。

Stance: Musubidachi.
Hands: Stretch both arms with hands putting on both sides of the thighs.

立ち方／結び立ち。

Stance: Musubidachi.

立ち方／結び立ち。
手の動作／両手を伸ばし、大腿部外側に付ける。

Stance: Musubidachi.
Hands: Stretch both arms with hands putting on both sides of the thighs.

●挙動の分解　Kumite in detail

途中動作	用意	用意

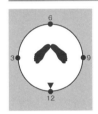	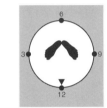	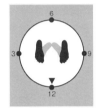

足の動作／そのまま。
立ち方／結び立ち。
手の動作／両掌を重ね、水月前に上げる。
＊次の用意まで連続して行う。

Feet: Keep in the same position as ❸.
Stance: Musubidachi.
Hands: Put both hands together and hold them in front of the solar plexus.
＊ Continuous movement to ❺.

足の動作／そのまま。
立ち方／結び立ち。
手の動作／両手は開手のまま、右甲に左掌を重ねて、床を押すように下腹部前に構える。

Feet: Keep in the same position as ❸.
Stance: Musubidachi.
Hands: With both hands open, lay the palm of the left on the back of the right hand and hold it in front of the lower abdomen as if you pushed down the floor.

足の動作／上足底を軸に両踵を平行に開く。
立ち方／平行立ち。
手の動作／両拳は握り、体の両側に開く。手の甲は外向きにする。

Feet: Open both heels parallel with pivoting on upper soles.
Stance: Heikodachi.
Hands: Hold both fists along the side of the body. The back of the hand is outward.

心波

061

移行動作	途中動作	1 挙動
	 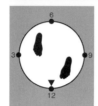	 
Transition Movement	Transition Movement	足の動作／右足を右斜後方に引く。 立ち方／左三戦立ち。 手の動作／左上段繰り受け。右拳は脇に引く。 Feet: Pull the right foot to the right oblique back. Stance: Left Sanchindachi. Hands: Do Left Jodan Kuri-uke. Pull the right fist to armpit.

● 挙動の分解　Kumite in detail

2 挙動　　　3 挙動　　　4 挙動

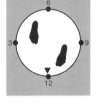
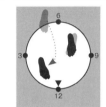
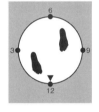

足の動作／そのまま。
立ち方／左三戦立ち。
手の動作／右中段逆突き。左拳は脇に引く。

Feet: Keep in the same position as ❾．
Stance: Left Sanchindachi.
Hands: Do Right Chudan Gyaku-zuki. Pull the left fist to armpit.

足の動作／右足を一歩前方へ。
立ち方／右三戦立ち。
手の動作／右上段繰り受け。

Feet: Step forward with the right foot.
Stance: Right Sanchindachi.
Hands: Do Right Jodan Kuri-uke.

足の動作／そのまま。
立ち方／右三戦立ち。
手の動作／左中段逆突き。右拳は脇に引く。

Feet: Keep in the same position as ⓫．
Stance: Right Sanchindachi.
Hands: Do Left Chudan Gyaku-zuki. Pull the right fist to armpit.

心波

1挙動〜10挙動

相手の上段突きに対し、右足を引き左上段繰り受けを行う。

Block your opponent's Jodan Zuki by drawing back your right leg and performing a Left Jodan Kuri-uke.

相手の突き手を取り、引きながら右拳にて中段逆突きを行う。

Catch your opponent's striking hand, and, while pulling, perform a Chudan Gyaku-zuki with your right fist.

（反対側から見たところ）

(the view from the other side)

5 挙動	6 挙動	7 挙動
 ⑬	 ⑭	 ⑮
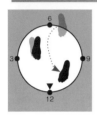		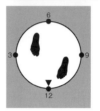

足の動作／左足を一歩前方へ。
立ち方／左三戦立ち。
手の動作／左上段繰り受け。

Feet: Step forward with the left foot.
Stance: Left Sanchindachi.
Hands: Do Left Jodan Kuri-uke.

足の動作／そのまま。
立ち方／左三戦立ち。
手の動作／右中段逆突き。（6〜8挙動は3連突き）

Feet: Keep in the same position as ⑬.
Stance: Left Sanchindachi.
Hands: Do Right Chudan Gyaku-zuki.
(6 to 8 movements are three consecutive Tsuki)

足の動作／そのまま。
立ち方／左三戦立ち。
手の動作／左中段突き。

Feet: Keep in the same position as ⑬.
Stance: Left Sanchindachi.
Hands: Do Left Chudan Zuki.

●挙動の分解　Kumite in detail

8 挙動

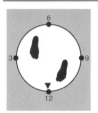

足の動作／そのまま。
立ち方／左三戦立ち。
手の動作／右中段逆突き。

Feet: Keep in the same position as ⑩.
Stance: Left Sanchindachi.
Hands: Do Right Chudan Gyaku-zuki.

9 挙動

足の動作／右中段前蹴り。
手の動作／そのまま。

Feet: Do Right Chudan Mae-geri.
Hands: Keep in the same position as ⑬.

10 挙動

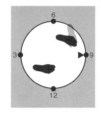

足の動作／蹴った足を引き、9時方向を向く。
立ち方／左三戦立ち。
手の動作／左上段繰り受け。右拳は脇に引く。

Feet: Pull back the kicked leg and turn the body in the direction of 9 o'clock.
Stance: Left Sanchindachi.
Hands: Do Left Jodan Kuri-uke. Pull the right fist to armpit.

心波

11 挙動　　12 挙動　　13 挙動

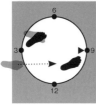  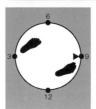

足の動作／右足を前方へ運ぶ。
立ち方／右前屈立ち。
手の動作／右開手中段縦肘当て。左拳は握って脇に引く。

Feet: Step forward with the right foot.
Stance: Right Zenkutsudachi.
Hands: Do Right Kaishu Chudan Tatehiji-ate. Pull the left fist to armpit.

足の動作／そのまま。
立ち方／右前屈立ち。
手の動作／左中段逆突き。右拳は脇に引く。（12～13挙動は連続）

Feet: Keep in the same position as ⑲.
Stance: Right Zenkutsudachi.
Hands: Do Left Chudan Gyaku-zuki. Pull the right fist to armpit.(12 to 13 movements are continuous)

足の動作／そのまま。
立ち方／右前屈立ち。
手の動作／右中段突き。左拳は脇に引く。

Feet: Keep in the same position as ⑲.
Stance: Right Zenkutsudachi.
Hands: Do Right Chudan Zuki. Pull the left fist to armpit.

●挙動の分解　Kumite in detail

相手の上段突きに対し、右足を引き左上段繰り受けを行う。

Block your opponent's Jodan Zuki by drawing back your right leg and performing a Jodan Kuri-uke.

中段前蹴りを行う。

Perform a Chudan Mae-geri.

蹴った足を下ろし、右中段肘当てを行う。

Lower your kicking leg and perform a Right Chudan Hiji-ate.

066

14 挙動　　　　　　15 挙動　　　　　　16 挙動

足の動作／右足を左方に運び、左廻り
で3時方向に向く。
立ち方／左三戦立ち
手の動作／左上段繰り受け

Feet: Bring the right foot to the left, turn the body counterclockwise in the direction of 3 o'clock.
Stance: Left Sanchindachi.
Hands: Do Left Jodan Kuri-uke.

足の動作／そのまま。
立ち方／左三戦立ち。
手の動作／右中段逆突き。左拳は脇に引く。

Feet: Keep in the same position as ㉒.
Stance: Left Sanchindachi.
Hands: Do Right Chudan Gyaku-zuki. Pull the left fist to armpit.

足の動作／右足を一歩前方へ。
立ち方／右三戦立ち。
手の動作／右上段繰り受け。

Feet: Step forward with the right foot.
Stance: Right Sanchindachi.
Hands: Do Right Jodan Kuri-uke.

心波

067

17 挙動　　　18 挙動　　　19 挙動

㉕

㉖

㉗

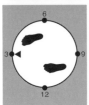

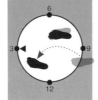

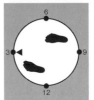

足の動作／そのまま。
立ち方／右三戦立ち。
手の動作／左中段逆突き。右拳は脇に引く。

Feet: Keep in the same position as ㉔.
Stance: Right Sanchindachi.
Hands: Do Left Chudan Gyaku-zuki. Pull the right fist to armpit.

足の動作／左足を一歩前方へ。
立ち方／左三戦立ち。
手の動作／左上段繰り受け。右拳は脇に引く。

Feet: Step forward with the left foot.
Stance: Left Sanchindachi.
Hands: Do Left Jodan Kuri-uke. Pull the right fist to armpit.

足の動作／そのまま。
立ち方／左三戦立ち。
手の動作／右中段逆突き。左拳は脇に引く。（19〜21挙動は3連突き）

Feet: Keep in the same position as ㉖.
Stance: Left Sanchindachi.
Hands: Do Right Chudan Gyaku-zuki. Pull the left fist to armpit.(19 to 21 movements are three consecutive Tsuki)

●挙動の分解　Kumite in detail

068

20 挙動　　　21 挙動　　　22 挙動

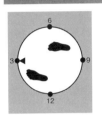 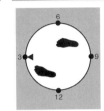 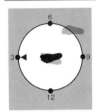

足の動作／そのまま。
立ち方／左三戦立ち
手の動作／左中段突き。右拳は脇に引く。

Feet: Keep in the same position as ㉖ .
Stance: Left Sanchindachi.
Hands: Do Left Chudan Zuki. Pull the right fist to armpit.

足の動作／そのまま。
立ち方／左三戦立ち。
手の動作／右中段逆突き。左拳は脇に引く。

Feet: Keep in the same position as ㉖ .
Stance: Left Sanchindachi.
Hands: Do Right Chudan Gyaku-zuki. Pull the left fist to armpit.

足の動作／右中段前蹴り。
手の動作／そのまま。

Feet: Do Right Chudan Mae-geri.
Hands: Keep in the same position as ㉙ .

心波

23 挙動

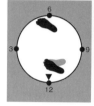 

足の動作／蹴った右足を右（6時）方向へ引く。体面は3時方向。
立ち方／後屈立ち。
手の動作／左下段払い。右小手を垂直にして肘関節を曲げ、右拳は耳の高さに構える。

Feet: Pull back the kicked leg in the direction of 6 o'clock. The front of the body is facing in the direction of 3 o'clock.
Stance: Right Kokutsudachi.
Hands: Do Left Gedan Barai. Bend the right elbow joint, make the right forearm vertical, hold the right fist at the height of your ears.

24 挙動

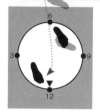

足の動作／右足を前方（12時方向）へ一歩運ぶ。
立ち方／右前屈立ち。
手の動作／両拳槌を中段に打ち込む。（両拳の甲が下）

Feet: Bring the right foot in the direction of 12 o'clock.
Stance: Right Zenkutsudachi.
Hands: Drive the both Kentsui into Chudan.(Back of the hands are facing down)

25 挙動

足の動作／右足を軸に左足を引き付けながら、左廻りで後方（6時方向）に向く。
立ち方／左猫足立ち。
手の動作／左上段繰り受け。右拳は脇に引く。

Feet: While pull back the left foot, turn the body counterclockwise in the direction of 6 o'clock with pivoting on the right foot.
Stance: Left Nekoashidachi.
Hands: Do Left Jodan Kuri-uke. Pull the right fist to armpit.

●挙動の分解　Kumite in detail

23挙動〜24挙動

相手の右中段前蹴りに対し、後屈立ち下段払いで受ける。

Parry your opponent's Right Chudan Mae-geri with a Gedan Barai in the Kokutsudachi stance.

前屈立ちとなり、両拳槌で相手の脇を打つ。

Assume the Zenkutsudachi stance and use both fists to strike both sides of your opponent with a Kentsui.

25挙動〜26挙動

相手の右上段突きに対し、猫足立ちになり上段繰り受けを行う。

Block your opponent's Right Jodan Zuki with a Jodan Kuri-uke in the Nekoashidachi stance.

中段逆突きを行う。

Perform a Chudan Gyaku-zuki.

26 挙動　　　27 挙動　　　28 挙動

  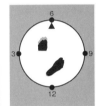  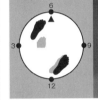 

足の動作／そのまま。
立ち方／左猫足立ち。
手の動作／右中段逆突き。左拳は脇に引く。

Feet: Keep in the same position as ㉝.
Stance: Left Nekoashidachi.
Hands: Do Right Chudan Gyaku-zuki. Pull the left fist to armpit.

足の動作／左足を手前に引く。
立ち方／左浮き足立ち。
手の動作／開手上段輪受け。

Feet: Pull the left leg backward.
Stance: Left Ukiashidachi.
Hands: Do Kaishu Jodan Wa-uke.

足の動作／左足を前方に運ぶ。
立ち方／左前屈立ち。
手の動作／両小拳頭を中段に打ち込む。
（縦拳で手の甲は外側を向く）

Feet: Bring the left foot forward.
Stance: Left Zenkutsudachi.
Hands: Drive the both Sho Kentou into Chudan.(Use Tateken with back of the hands are facing outward)

相手の右上段突きに対し、猫足立ちになり上段繰り受けを行う。

さらに左上段突きに対し、浮き足立ちとなり上段開手輪受けを行う。

前屈立ちとなり、相手の脇腹に両小拳頭を打ち込む。

Block your opponent's Right Jodan Zuki with a Jodan Kuri-uke in the Nekoashidachi stance.

Block the Left Jodan Zuki with a Jodan Kaishu Wa-uke in the Ukiashidachi stance.

Assume the Zenkutsudachi stance and use both fists to strike your opponent's sides with both Sho-Kentou.

29 挙動

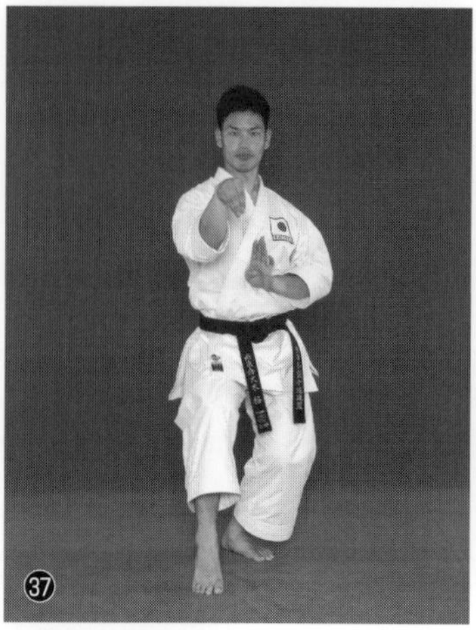

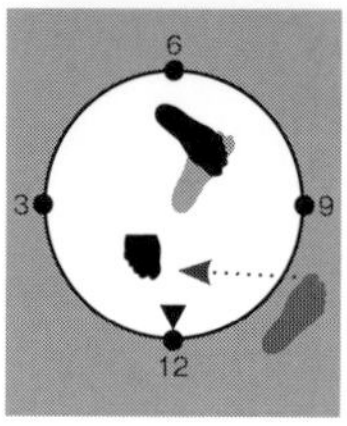

足の動作／左足を軸に右廻りで前方（12 時方向）に向く。
立ち方／右猫足立ち。
手の動作／右弧拳にて胸部前に跳ね上げ、左中段掌底押さえ受け。

Feet: Face clockwise in the direction of 12 o'clock with pivoting on the left foot.
Stance: Right Nekoashidachi.
Hands: Strike up Right Koken in front of the chest and do Left Chudan Shote Osae-uke .

30 挙動

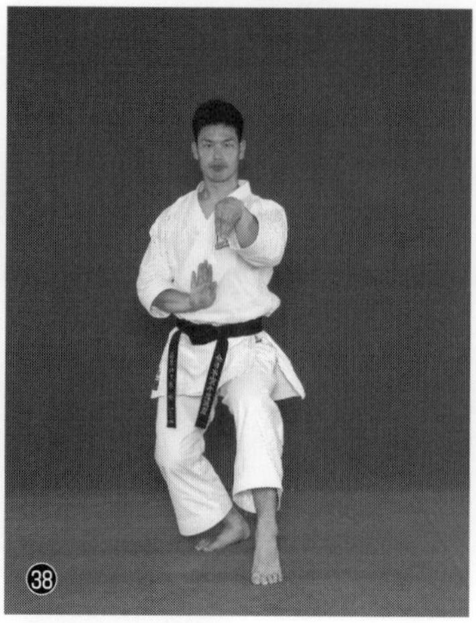

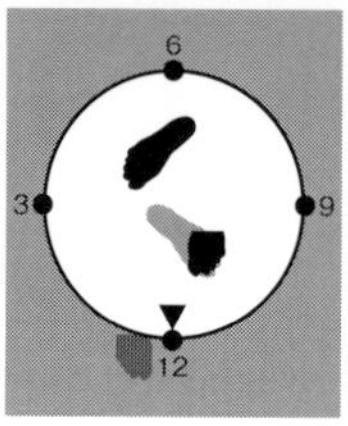

足の動作／右足を後方へ引く。
立ち方／左猫足立ち。
手の動作／左弧拳。右中段掌底押さえ受け。

Feet: Pull the right foot backward.
Stance: Left Nekoashidachi.
Hands: Do Left Koken and Right Chudan Shote Osae-uke

止めへの移行動作

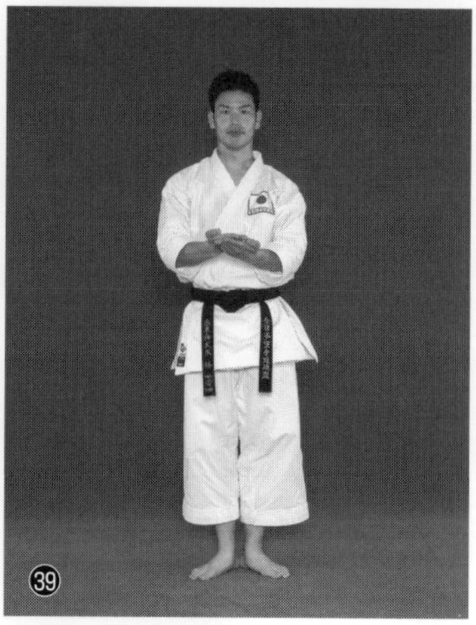

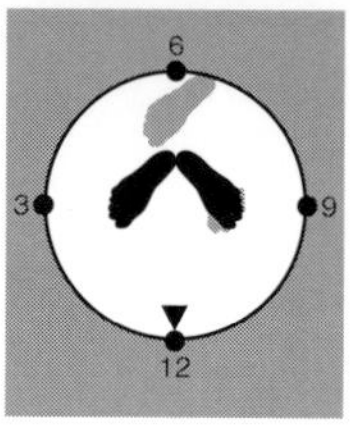

足の動作／右足を左足に引き寄せる。
立ち方／結び立ち。
手の動作／両開手を重ね、水月前に上げる。
＊止めまで連続して行う。

Feet: Pull the right foot to the left foot.
Stance: Musubidachi.
Hands: Put both hands together and hold them in front of the solar plexus.
＊ Continuous movement to ㊵ .

●挙動の分解　Kumite in detail

29挙動～30挙動

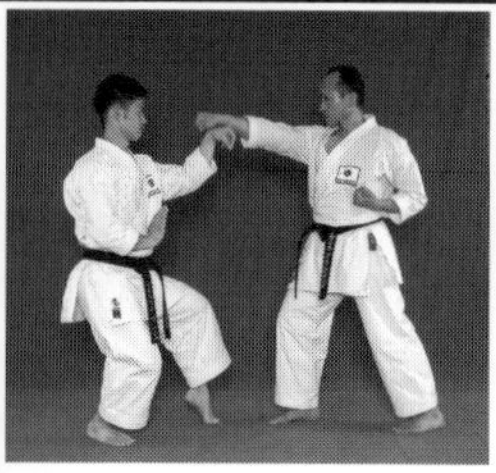

相手の右上段突きに対し、猫足立ちになり左孤拳にて受ける。

Parry your opponent's Right Jodan Zuki with a Left Koken in the Nekoashidachi stance.

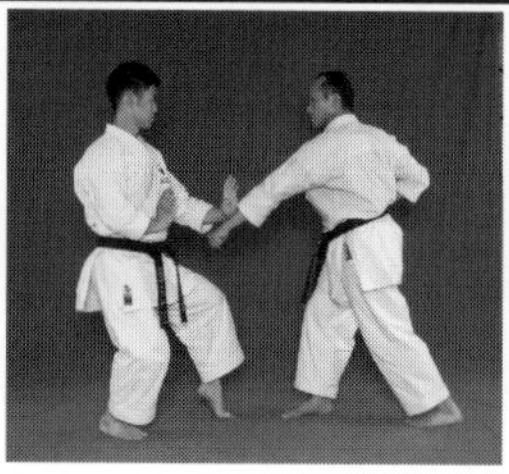

相手の左中段逆突きに対し、左掌底で受ける。

Parry your opponent's Left Chudan Gyaku-zuki with your Left Shotei.

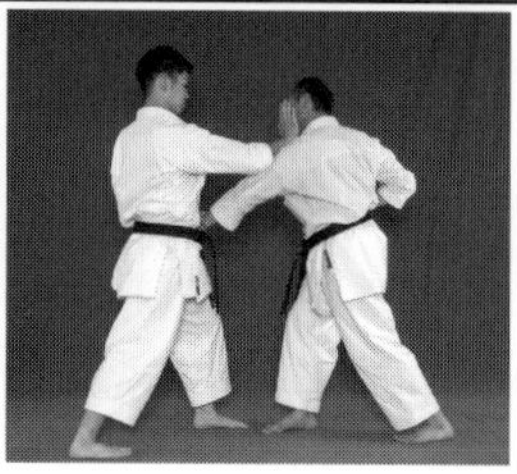

右掌底で相手の上段を攻撃する。

Strike your opponent's Jodan with your Right Shotei.

止め	気を付けの姿勢	礼

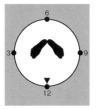	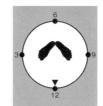	

足の動作／そのまま。
立ち方／結び立ち。
手の動作／両手は開手のまま、右甲に左掌を重ねて、床を押さえるように下腹部前に構える。

Feet: Keep in the same position as ㊴.
Stance: Musubidachi.
Hands: With both hands open, lay the palm of the left on the back of the right hand and hold it in front of the lower abdomen as if you pushed down the floor.

足の動作／そのまま。
立ち方／結び立ち。
手の動作／両開手を大腿部外側へ付ける。

Feet: Keep in the same position as ㊴.
Stance: Musubidachi.
Hands: Stretch both arms with hands putting on both sides of the thighs.

心波

気を付けの姿勢

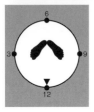

● 挙動の分解　Kumite in detail

心波

アーナンコウ

　アーナンコウは、 喜屋武朝徳翁の父朝扶が息子朝徳に伝授したという説と、 喜屋武朝徳翁が台湾人に指導を受け、 研究改良し伝えたとの二説があります。
　安定した立ち方と素早く切れの良い連続技が要求され、 更に全体として緩急変化の表現を要求されます。

There are two theories as to the origin of Ananko. The first is that it was passed down to master Kyan Chotoku from his father, Chobu. The second is that master Kyan Chotoku perfected techniques that he learned from a Taiwanese martial artist.
Ananko demands a stable pose and quick, successive techniques, as well as an overall flexibility in switching between fast and slow movements.

ANANKO

気を付けの姿勢	礼	直立	用意	1挙動	2挙動
 ①	 ②	 ③	 ④	 ⑤	 ⑥

9挙動	途中動作	途中動作	10挙動	11挙動	12挙動
 ⑬	 ⑭	 ⑮	 ⑯	 ⑰	 ⑱

19挙動	20挙動	21挙動	22挙動	23挙動	24挙動
 ㉕	 ㉖	 ㉗	 ㉘	 ㉙	 ㉚

29挙動	上段裏打ちしたところ	30挙動	31挙動	32挙動	33挙動
 ㊲	 ㊳	 ㊴	 ㊵	 ㊶	 ㊷

 止め
 気を付けの姿勢
 礼
 気を付けの姿勢

アーナンコウ

気を付けの姿勢	礼	直立

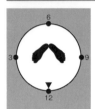		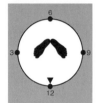

立ち方／結び立ち
手の動作／両手を伸ばし、大腿部外側に付ける。

Stance: Musubidachi.
Hands: Stretch both arms with hands putting on both sides of the thighs.

立ち方／結び立ち。

Stance: Musubidachi.

立ち方／結び立ち。
手の動作／両手を伸ばし、大腿部外側に付ける。

Stance: Musubidachi.
Hands: Stretch both arms with hands putting on both sides of the thighs.

● 挙動の分解　Kumite in detail

用意　　　　　　　1 挙動　　　　　　　2 挙動

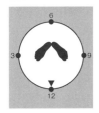
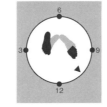

足の動作／そのまま
立ち方／結び立ち。
手の動作／左手を上に両掌を重ね、下腹部前に構える。

Feet: Keep in the same position as ❸.
Stance: Musubidachi.
Hands: Open both hands and hold them in front of the lower abdomen with the left hand putting on the right hand.

足の動作／左足を10時半方向へ運び左猫足立ち。
立ち方／左猫足立ち。
手の動作／左中段手刀受け。右開手で水月前に構える。

Feet: Bring the left foot in the direction of 10:30 o'clock to Left Nekoashidachi.
Stance: Left Nekoashidachi.
Hands: Do Left Chudan Shuto-uke. Hold the right open hand in front of the solar plexus.

足の動作／左足を軸に右足を1時半方向へ運ぶ。
立ち方／右猫足立ち。
手の動作／右中段手刀受け。左開手で水月前に構える。

Feet: Bring the right foot in the direction of 1:30 o'clock pivoting on the left foot.
Stance: Right Nekoashidachi.
Hands: Do Right Chudan Shuto-uke. Hold the left open hand in front of the solar plexus.

アーナンコウ

相手の中段追い突きに対し、左足を引いて左後方に転身し、右中段手刀受け。

Block your opponent's Chudan Oi-zuki by pulling back your left leg to shift your body to the rear left and doing a Right Chudan Shuto-uke.

左中段逆突きで極める。

Finish with a Left Chudan Gyaku-zuki.

3 挙動	4 挙動	5 挙動

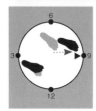	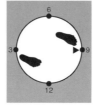	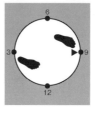

足の動作／右足を軸に左足を9時方向へ運ぶ。
立ち方／左前屈立ち。
手の動作／左中段横受け。右拳は脇に引く。
＊3挙動～5挙動連続動作

Feet: Bring the left foot in the direction of 9 o'clock pivoting on the right foot.
Stance: Left Zenkutsudachi.
Hands: Do Left Chudan Yoko-uke.
＊3 to 5 movements are continuous.

足の動作／そのまま
立ち方／左前屈立ち
手の動作／右中段逆突き。左拳は脇に引く。

Feet: Keep in the same position as ❼.
Stance: Left Zenkutsudachi.
Hands: Do Right Chudan Gyaku-zuki. Pull the left fist to armpit.

足の動作／そのまま
立ち方／左前屈立ち。
手の動作／左中段順突き。右拳は脇に引く。

Feet: Keep in the same position as ❼.
Stance: Left Zenkutsudachi.
Hands: Do Left Chudan Jun-zuki. Pull the right fist to armpit.

●挙動の分解　Kumite in detail

相手の右中段追い突きに対し、右足を引いて右後方に転身し、左中段横受け。

Block your opponent's Right Chudan Oi-zuki by pulling back your right leg to shift your body to the rear right and doing a Left Chudan Yoko-uke.

さらに相手の左中段逆突きに対し、右突き受けを行う。

Block your opponent's Left Chudan Gyaku-zuki with a Right Tsuki-uke.

さらに左中段突きで極める。

Finish with a Left Chudan Zuki.

6 挙動　　　　7 挙動　　　　8 挙動

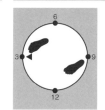
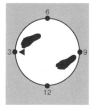

足の動作／左足を軸に右回りで右足を3時方向へ運ぶ。
立ち方／右前屈立ち
手の動作／右中段横受け。左拳は脇に引く。
＊6挙動〜8挙動連続動作

Feet: Turn the body clockwise and bring the right foot in the direction of 3 o'clock pivoting on the left foot.
Stance: Right Zenkutsudachi.
Hands: Do Right Chudan Yoko-uke. Pull the left fist to armpit.
＊ 6 to 8 movements are continuous.

足の動作／そのまま。
立ち方／右前屈立ち。
手の動作／左中段逆突き。右拳は脇に引く。

Feet: Keep in the same position as ⓾.
Stance: Right Zenkutsudachi.
Hands: Do Left Chudan Gyaku-zuki. Pull the right fist to armpit.

足の動作／そのまま
立ち方／右前屈立ち
手の動作／右中段順突き。左拳は脇に引く。

Feet: Keep in the same position as ⓾.
Stance: Right Zenkutsudachi.
Hands: Do Right Chudan Jun-zuki. Pull the left fist to armpit.

アーナンコウ

9 挙動	途中動作	途中動作

⑬	⑭	⑮
	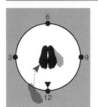	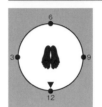

足の動作／左足を6時方向に引く。
立ち方／右前屈立ち。
手の動作／右中段横打ち。左拳は脇に引く。

Feet: Pull the left foot in the direction of 6 o'clock.
Stance: Right Zenkutsudachi.
Hands: Do Right Chudan Yoko-uchi. Pull the left fist to armpit.

足の動作／右足を左足の方へ引く。
立ち方／閉足立ち。
手の動作／右拳を左から下段掬い受け。

Feet: Pull the right foot to the left foot.
Stance: Heisokudachi.
Hands: Do Gedan Sukui-uke from the left with a right fist.

●挙動の分解　Kumite in detail

9挙動〜10挙動

相手の右中段追い突きに対し、左足を引いて右中段横打ち。

Block your opponent's Right Chudan Oi-zuki by pulling back your left leg and doing a Right Chudan Yoko-uchi.

相手の左中段前蹴りを掬い受け。

Perform a Sukui-uke against your opponent's Left Chudan Mae-geri.

相手を倒して極める。

Finish by throwing your opponent down.

10 挙動　　　11 挙動　　　12 挙動

足の動作／そのまま。
立ち方／閉足立ち。
手の動作／右拳はそのまま回して甲を上にして左脇構え。左拳は脇に引く。

Feet: Keep in the same position as ⑮.
Stance: Heisokudachi.
Hands: Drawing a circle the right fist with the back upward put it in the left armpit. Pull the left fist to armpit.

足の動作／右足を 12 時方向へ運ぶ。
立ち方／右猫足立ち。
手の動作／上段輪受け。

Feet: Bring the right foot in direction of the 12 o'clock.
Stance: Right Nekoashidachi.
Hands: Do Jodan Wa-uke.

足の動作／立ち方はそのままで寄り足にて 12 時方向に踏み込む。
立ち方／右猫足立ち。
手の動作／両拳中段拳槌打ち。

Feet: Step forward with the same position in the direction of 12 o'clock (Yoriashi).
Stance: Right Nekoashidachi.
Hands: Do Ryoken Chudan Kentsui-uchi.

アーナンコウ

相手の右上段追い突きを左足を引いて猫足立ちになり上段輪受け。

Pull the left foot backwards and Block your opponent's Right Jodan Oi-zuki with a Jodan Wa-uke in the Nekoashidachi stance.

右足を踏み込み、両拳槌にて相手の脇腹を打つ。

Step forward with your right leg and, with both fists, perform a Kentsui strike on your opponent's sides.

下がる相手に対し、右中段突きで極める。

Use a Right Chudan Zuki to finish your withdrawing opponent.

13 挙動	14 挙動	15 挙動

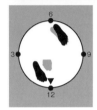		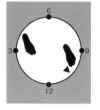

足の動作／右足を12時方向へ運ぶ。
立ち方／右前屈立ち。
手の動作／右中段追い突き。左拳は脇に引く。

Feet: Step forward the right foot in the direction of 12 o'clock.
Stance: Right Zenkutsudachi.
Hands: Do Right Chudan Oi-zuki. Pull the left fist to armpit.

足の動作／左足を10時半方向へ運ぶ。
立ち方／左前屈立ち。
手の動作／左中段横受け。右拳は脇へ引く。
＊14挙動〜16挙動連続動作

Feet: Bring the left foot in the direction of 10:30 o'clock.
Stance: Left Zenkutsudachi.
Hands: Do Left Chudan Yoko-uke. Pull the right fist to armpit.
＊14 to 16 movements are continuous.

足の動作／そのまま。
立ち方／左前屈立ち。
手の動作／右中段逆突き。左拳は脇へ引く。

Feet: Keep in the same position as ⑳.
Stance: Left Zenkutsudachi.
Hands: Do Right Chudan Gyaku-zuki. Pull the left fist to armpit.

●挙動の分解　Kumite in detail

相手の右中段追い突きに対し、右後方に転身して前屈立ちとなり左中段横受け。

Block your opponent's Right Chudan Oi-zuki by pulling back your right leg to shift your body to the rear right and doing a Left Chudan Yoko-uke.

さらに相手の左中段逆突きに対し、右突き受けを行う。

Block your opponent's Left Chudan Gyaku-zuki with a Right Tsuki-uke.

素早く左上段突きを行う。

Quickly do a Left Jodan Zuki.

16 挙動　　　17 挙動　　　18 挙動

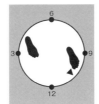
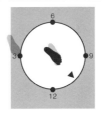

足の動作／そのまま。
立ち方／左前屈立ち。
手の動作／左上段順突き。右拳は脇へ引く。

Feet: Keep in the same position as ⑳.
Stance: Left Zenkutsudachi.
Hands: Do Left Jodan Jun-zuki. Pull the right fist to armpit.

足の動作／そのまま。
立ち方／左前屈立ち。
手の動作／左中段横打ちをゆっくり行う。右拳は脇へ引く。

Feet: Keep in the same position as ⑳.
Stance: Left Zenkutsudachi.
Hands: Do Left Chudan Yoko-uchi slowly. Pull the right fist to armpit.

足の動作／右中段前蹴り。
手の動作／そのまま。

Feet: Do Right Chudan Mae-geri.
Hands: Keep in the same position as ㉓.

アーナンコウ

17挙動〜19挙動

相手の右中段突きに対し、左中段横打ち行う。

Block your opponent's Right Chudan Zuki with a Right Chudan Yoko-uchi.

右中段前蹴りで反撃。

Counter with a Right Chudan Mae-geri.

右中段逆突きで極める。

Finish with a Right Chudan Gyaku-zuki.

089

19 挙動	20 挙動	21 挙動

	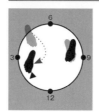	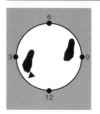

足の動作／蹴った右足を4時半方向へ引く。
立ち方／左前屈立ち。
手の動作／右中段逆突き。左拳は脇へ引く。

Feet: Pull the right foot in the direction of 4:30 o'clock.
Stance: Left Zenkutsudachi.
Hands: Do Right Chudan Gyaku-zuki. Pull the left fist to armpit.

足の動作／右足を1時半方向へ運ぶ。
立ち方／右前屈立ち。
手の動作／右中段横受け。左拳は脇へ引く。
＊20挙動〜22挙動連続動作

Feet: Bring the right foot in the direction of 1:30 o'clock.
Stance: Right Zenkutsudachi.
Hands: Do Right Chudan Yoko-Uke. Pull the left fist to armpit.
＊ 20 to 22 movements are continuous.

足の動作／そのまま。
立ち方／右前屈立ち。
手の動作／左中段逆突き。右拳は脇へ引く。

Feet: Keep in the same position as ㉖.
Stance: Right Zenkutsudachi.
Hands: Do Left Chudan Gyaku-zuki. Pull the right fist to armpit.

●挙動の分解　Kumite in detail

22 挙動　　　　23 挙動　　　　24 挙動

足の動作／そのまま。
立ち方／右前屈立ち。
手の動作／右上段順突き。左拳は脇へ引く。

Feet: Keep in the same position as ㉖.
Stance: Right Zenkutsudachi.
Hands: Do Right Jodan Jun-zuki. Pull the left fist to armpit.

足の動作／そのまま。
立ち方／右前屈立ち。
手の動作／右中段横打ちをゆっくり行う。左拳は脇へ引く。

Feet: Keep in the same position as ㉖.
Stance: Right Zenkutsudachi.
Hands: Do Right Chudan Yoko-uchi slowly. Pull the left fist to armpit.

足の動作／左中段前蹴り。
手の動作／そのまま。

Feet: Do Left Chudan Mae-geri.
Hands: Keep in the same position as ㉙.

アーナンコウ

25 挙動	26 挙動	27 挙動

	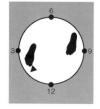	

足の動作／蹴った左足を7時半方向へ引く。
立ち方／右前屈立ち。
手の動作／左中段逆突き。右拳は脇へ引く。

Feet: Pull the left foot in the direction of 7:30 o'clock.
Stance: RIght Zenkutsudachi.
Hands: Do Left Chudan Gyaku-zuki. Pull the right fist to armpit.

足の動作／そのまま。
立ち方／右前屈立ち。
手の動作／左手刀で12時方向へ左開手下段払い。

Feet: Keep in the same position as ㉛.
Stance: Right Zenkutsudachi.
Hands: Do Left Kaisyu Gedan Barai in the direction of 12 o'clock.

足の動作／左足を軸に右足を12時方向へ運ぶ。
立ち方／四股立ち。
手の動作／左掌に右中段肘当てを行う。

Feet: Bring the right foot in the direction of 12 o'clock pivoting on the left foot.
Stance: Shikodachi.
Hands: Do Right Chudan Hiji-ate on left palm.

●挙動の分解　Kumite in detail

26挙動〜28挙動

相手の右中段追い突きに対し、左足を引いて前屈立ちとなり、左手刀下段払い。

Block your opponent's Right Chudan Oi-zuki by pulling back your left leg and doing a Left Shuto Gedan Barai in the Zenkutsudachi stance.

素早く肘当てを行う。

Quickly perform an elbow strike.

(反対から見たところ)

(the view from the other side)

腰を切って左後屈立ちとなり、右拳槌打ちで下段急所へ攻撃する。

Twist hips into Left Kokutsudachi stance and strike the crotch with Right Kentsui-uchi.

28 挙動　　　　移行動作（6時方向から）　　　移行動作（6時方向から）

足の動作／左右足の上足底を軸に回転し6時方向へ向く。
立ち方／左前屈立ち。
手の動作／左下段払い。右下段拳槌打ち。

Feet: Turn the body counterclockwise in the direction of 6 o'clock pivoting on the upper soles.
Stance: Left Zenkutsudachi.
Hands: Do Left Gedan Barai and Right Gedan Kentsui-uchi.

Transition Movement
(The view from 6 o'clock)

Transition Movement
(The view from 6 o'clock)

アーナンコウ

（反対から見たところ）

(the view from the other side)

28挙動〜30挙動

相手の中段前蹴りに対し、下段払いを行う。

Block your opponent's Chudan Mae-geri with a Gedan Barai.

相手の右上段突きに対し、上段繰り受け。

Block your opponent's Right Jodan Zuki with a Jodan Kuri-uke.

右上段裏打ちで極める。

Finish with a Right Jodan Ura-uchi.

093

29 挙動　　上段裏打ちしたところ　　30 挙動

足の動作／そのまま。
立ち方／左前屈立ち。
手の動作／左上段繰り受け。右拳はそのまま。

Feet: Keep in the same position as ㉞.
Stance: Left Zenkutsudachi.
Hands: Do Left Jodan Kuri-uke. The right fist is as it is.

足の動作／右足を6時方向へ大きく運ぶ。
立ち方／右交差立ち。
手の動作／右上段裏打ち。左拳は脇に引く。

Feet: Bring the right foot greatly in the direction of 6 o'clock.
Stance: Right Kosadachi.
Hands: Do Right Jodan Ura-uchi. Pull the left fist to armpit.

足の動作／そのまま。
立ち方／右交差立ち。
手の動作／右拳を肩の高さにする。左拳はそのまま。

Feet: Keep in the same position as ㊳.
Stance: Right Kosadachi.
Hands: Set the right fist to the height of the shoulder. Left fist as it is.

●挙動の分解　Kumite in detail

31 挙動　　32 挙動　　33 挙動

 　 　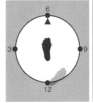

足の動作／左足、右足を12時方向へ引く。
立ち方／右猫足立ち。
手の動作／右中段横打ち。左拳は左脇に引く。

Feet: Pull both feet in the direction of 12 o'clock.
Stance: RIght Nekoashidachi.
Hands: Do Right Chudan Yoko-uchi. Pull the left fist to armpit.

足の動作／6時方向へ左足を右足前に運ぶ。
手の動作／そのまま。

Feet: Bring the left foot in the direction of 6 o'clock, and put it in front of the right foot.
Hands: Keep in the same position as ④ .

足の動作／右中段前蹴り。
手の動作／そのまま。

Feet: Do Right Chudan Mae-geri.
Hands: Keep in the same position as ④ .

アーナンコウ

31挙動〜35挙動

相手の右中段追い突きに対し左足を引いて猫足立ちになり、右中段横打ち。

Block your opponent's Right Chudan Oi-zuki by pulling back your left leg and doing a Right Chudan Yoko-uchi in the Nekoashidachi stance.

右中段前蹴りを行う。

Do a Right Chudan Mae-geri.

左中段突きに対し、右下段払い。

Block the Left Chudan Zuki with a Gedan Barai.

素早く左中段逆突きで極める。

Quickly finish with a Left Chudan Gyaku-zuki.

34 挙動　　　35 挙動　　　36 挙動

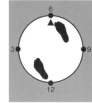 　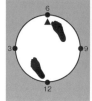 　

足の動作／蹴った右足を6時方向へ下ろす。
立ち方／右前屈立ち。
手の動作／右下段払い。左拳は脇へ引く。

Feet: Put down the rightt foot in the direction of 6 o'clock.
Stance: RIght Zenkutsudachi.
Hands: Do Right Gedan Barai. Pull the left fist to armpit.

足の動作／そのまま。
立ち方／右前屈立ち。
手の動作／左中段逆突き。右拳は脇へ引く。

Feet: Keep in the same position as ㊸.
Stance: RIght Zenkutsudachi.
Hands: Do Left Chudan Gyaku-zuki. Pull the right fist to armpit.

足の動作／右足を12時方向へ引く。
立ち方／右猫足立ち。
手の動作／右中段横打ち。左拳は左脇に引く。

Feet: Pull the right foot in the direction of 12 o'clock.
Stance: RIght Nekoashidachi.
Hands: Do Right Chudan Yoko-uchi. Pull the left fist to armpit.

●挙動の分解　Kumite in detail

相手の右中段追い突きに対し左足を引いて猫足立ちになり、右中段横打ち。
Block your opponent's Right Chudan Oi-zuki by pulling back your left leg and doing a Right Chudan Yoko-uchi in the Nekoashidachi stance.

さらに相手の左中段前蹴りを掬い止め。
Stop your opponent's Left Chudan Mae-geri with a Sukui-dome.

中段逆突きで極める。
Finish with a Chudan Gyaku-zuki.

移行動作	37 挙動	38 挙動

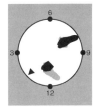		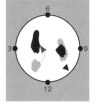
足の動作／左右足の上足底を中心に左廻りで1時半方向を向く。 手の動作／右下段掬い受けしながら。 Feet: Turn the body counterclockwise in the direction of 1:30 o'clock pivoting on the upper soles. Hands: Do Right Gedan Sukui-uke.	足の動作／左足を7時半方向へ引く。 立ち方／右猫足立ち。 手の動作／右手刀受け。左手は開手で水月前に構える。 Feet: Pull the left foot in the direction of 7 o'clock. Stance: RIght Nekoashidachi. Hands: Do Right Shuto-uke. Hold the hands to the solar plexus.	足の動作／右足を4時半方向へ引く。 立ち方／左猫足立ち。 手の動作／左手刀受け。右手は開手で水月前に構える。 Feet: Pull the right foot in the direction of 4:30 o'clock. Stance: Leftt Nekoashidachi. Hands: Do Left Shuto-uke. Hold the hands to the solar plexus.

アーナンコウ

相手の右中段追い突きに対し、左後方に引いて右猫足立ちになり右中段手刀受け。

Block your opponent's Right Chudan Oi-zuki by drawing back to the rear left and doing a Right Chudan Shuto-uke in the Right Nekoashidachi stance.

相手の右手を取り、相手の前脚の膝に足刀蹴り。

Take your opponent's right hand and kick the knee of their front leg with a Sokutou-geri.

さらに左上段逆突きで極める。

Finish with a Left Jodan Gyaku-zuki.

止め	気を付けの姿勢	礼

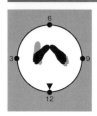	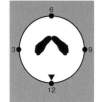	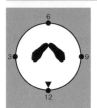

足の動作／左足を右足に引き寄せる。
立ち方／結び立ち。
手の動作／両開手を重ね、下腹部前に構える。

Feet: Pull the left foot to the right foot.
Stance: Musubidachi.
Hands: Put both hands on top and set in front of the lower abdomen.

足の動作／そのまま。
立ち方／結び立ち。
手の動作／両手を伸ばし、大腿部外側に付ける。

Feet: Keep in the same position as ㊾.
Stance: Musubidachi.
Hands: Stretch both arms with hands putting on both sides of the thighs.

● 挙動の分解　Kumite in detail

気を付けの姿勢

アーナンコウ

サイファ

　サイファは、 那覇手の系統の形であり、 三戦、 新生から進展させたような趣が見られる。

　単調な基本動作で構成されているが、 相手に手首や襟(肩口)を捕まえられたり、足払いあるいは足取りに来るのを外したり等、 護身術的技法が織り込まれた形である。

Saifa is a Kata of the Naha-te system. It developed from Sanchin and Shinsei.
Although it is composed of simplistic, foundational movements, it incorporates defensive techniques, such as escaping when your opponent has seized your wrist or collar and evading Ashi-barai and Ashi-tori attacks.

SAIFA

サイファ　形の流れ

気を付けの姿勢	礼	直立	途中動作	用意	用意
 ①	 ②	 ③	 ④	 ⑤	 ⑥

5 挙動	移行動作（3時方向から）	裏打ちしたところ	6 挙動	7 挙動	8 挙動
 ⑬	 ⑭	 ⑮	 ⑯	 ⑰	 ⑱

13 挙動	14 挙動	15 挙動	移行動作	途中動作	途中動作
 ㉕	 ㉖	 ㉗	 ㉘	 ㉙	 ㉚

途中動作（6時方向から）	20 挙動	21 挙動	22 挙動	移行動作	23 挙動
 ㊲	 ㊳	 ㊴	 ㊵	 ㊶	 ㊷

1 挙動	2 挙動	移行動作（9時方向から）	裏打ちしたところ	3 挙動	4 挙動
 ⑦	 ⑧	 ⑨	 ⑩	 ⑪	 ⑫
移行動作（9時方向から）	裏打ちしたところ	9 挙動	10 挙動	11 挙動	12 挙動
 ⑲	 ⑳	 ㉑	 ㉒	 ㉓	 ㉔
16 挙動	17 挙動	18 挙動	移行動作（9時方向から）	19 挙動	移行動作
 ㉛	 ㉜	 ㉝	 ㉞	 ㉟	 ㊱
24 挙動	25 挙動	移行動作	26 挙動	27 挙動	28 挙動
 ㊸	 ㊹	 ㊺	 ㊻	 ㊼	 ㊽

サイファ

止め

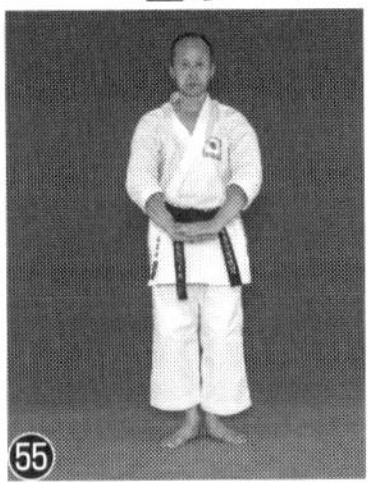

(55)

気を付けの姿勢

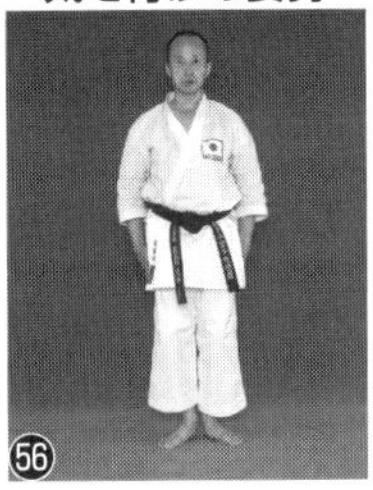

(56)

礼

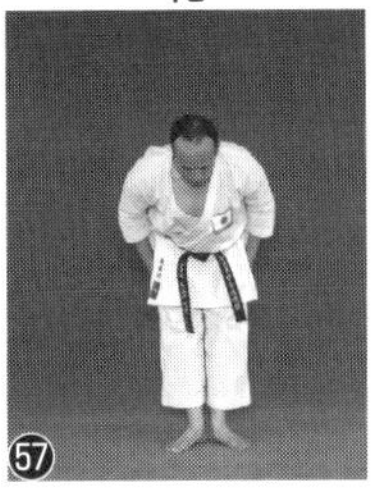

(57)

気を付けの姿勢

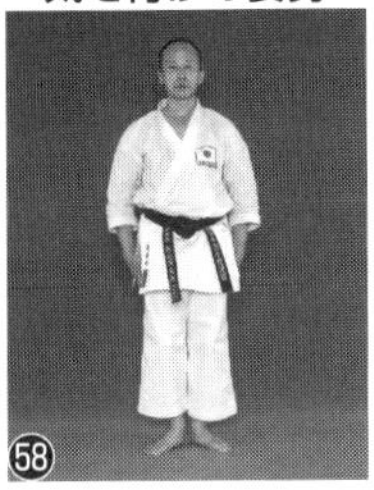

(58)

気を付けの姿勢	礼	直立

①	②	③
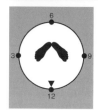	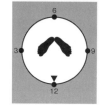	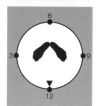

立ち方／結び立ち。
手の動作／両手を伸ばし、大腿部外側に付ける。

Stance: Musubidachi.
Hands: Stretch both arms with hands putting on both sides of the thighs.

立ち方／結び立ち。

Stance: Musubidachi.

立ち方／結び立ち。
手の動作／両手を伸ばし、大腿部外側に付ける。

Stance: Musubidachi.
Hands: Stretch both arms with hands putting on both sides of the thighs.

● 挙動の分解　Kumite in detail

途中動作	用意	用意

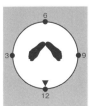	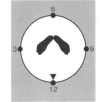	

足の動作／そのまま。
立ち方／結び立ち。
手の動作／両掌を重ね、水月前に上げる。
＊次の用意まで連続して行う。

Feet: Keep in the same position as ❸.
Stance: Musubidachi.
Hands: Open both hands and hold them in front of the solar plexus with the right hand putting on the left hand.
＊ Continue to the ❺ consecutive.

足の動作／そのまま。
立ち方／結び立ち。
手の動作／両手は開手のまま、右甲に左掌を重ねて、床を押すように下腹部前に構える。

Feet: Keep in the same position as ❸.
Stance: Musubidachi.
Hands: Open both hands and hold them in front of the lower abdomen as if pushed down the floor.

足の動作／上足底を軸に両踵を平行に開く。
立ち方／平行立ち。
手の動作／両拳は握り、体の両側に開く。

Feet: Set apart both heels parallel pivoting on the upper soles.
Stance: Heikoudachi.
Hands: Stretch both fists with hands putting on both sides of the thighs.

サイファ

1 挙動	2 挙動	移行動作（9時方向から）

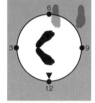		

足の動作／右足を右斜め前に一歩踏み出すと同時に、左足を右足に引き寄せ結び立ちになる。目付は12時方向を向く。
立ち方／結び立ち。
手の動作／右拳は握り甲を下に向け、左手は開手にて指を横にして左掌を右拳の正拳に添える。

Feet: Take the right foot one step to the right diagonally forward. At the same time, draws the left foot to the right foot to Musubidachi stance. The line of sight is at 12 o'clock.
Stance: Musubidachi.
Hands: Put the left palm sideways in front of the right Seiken with its back facing down.

足の動作／そのまま。
立ち方／結び立ち。
手の動作／右拳は体に沿って捻転させながら水月前に置く。手の甲は上に向ける。左掌は右拳に押されるようにして指を上向きに立て水月前。
＊体側まで引かないこと。

Feet: Keep in the same position as ❼.
Stance: Musubidachi.
Hands: Right fist is placed in front of the solar plexus while twisting along the body. The right fist's back is turned upward. Put the left palm with the finger facing up in front of the solar plexus and press the left palm with the right fist.
＊ Do not pull to the side.

Transition Movement
(view from 9 o'clock)

●挙動の分解　Kumite in detail

相手が左手で自分の右手を捕える。

Your opponent seizes your right hand with his left hand.

右肘を前方へ当てるように出す。

Thrust your right elbow forward to hit your opponent.

相手の右中段突きを左掌底で受けると同時に右上段裏打ちを極める。

Parry your opponent's Right Chudan Zuki with your Left Shotei, and, at the same time, finish with a Right Jodan Ura-uchi.

108

裏打ちしたところ	3 挙動	4 挙動

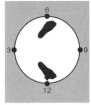 	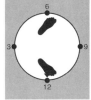	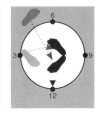

足の動作／右足を軸に左足を6時方向に引く。体の向きは9時方向。
立ち方／四股立ち。
手の動作／左掌にて右肘の方向へ押さえ受けをする。右拳にて12時方向へ上段裏拳打ちを行う。

Feet: Pull the left foot in the direction of 6 o'clock with pivoting on the right foot. The direction of the body is at 9 o'clock.
Stance: Sikodachi.
Hands: Do Osae-uke in the direction of the right elbow with the left hand. Do Jodan Uraken-uchi in the direction of 12 o'clock with right fist.

足の動作／そのまま。
立ち方／四股立ち。
手の動作／右拳を肩の高さに引く。

Feet: Keep in the same position as ⑩.
Stance: Shikodachi.
Hands: Pull the right fist to the height of the shoulder.

足の動作／左足を左斜め前に一歩踏み出すと同時に、右足を左足に引き寄せ結び立ちになる。目付は12時方向を向く。
立ち方／結び立ち。
手の動作／左拳は握り甲を下に向け、右手は開手にて指を横にして右掌を左拳の正拳に添える。

Feet: Take the left foot one step to the left diagonally forward. At the same time, draws the right foot to the left foot to Musubidachi stance. The line of sight is at 12 o'clock.
Stance: Musubidachi.
Hands: Put the right palm sideways in front of the left Seiken with its back facing down.

サイファ

5 挙動 　移行動作（3時方向から）　裏打ちしたところ

⑬　⑭　⑮

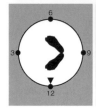  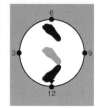

足の動作／そのまま。
立ち方／結び立ち。
手の動作／左拳は体に沿って捻転させながら水月前に置く。手の甲は上に向ける。右掌は左拳に押されるようにして指を上向きに立て水月前。
＊体側まで引かないこと。

Feet: Keep in the same position as ⑫.
Stance: Musubidachi.
Hands: Left fist is placed in front of the solar plexus while twisting along the body. The left fist's back is turned upward. Put the right palm with the finger facing up in front of the solar plexus and press the right palm with the left fist.

＊ Do not pull to the side.

Transition Movement

Transition Movement (Ura-uchi)

●挙動の分解　Kumite in detail

6 挙動　　　7 挙動　　　8 挙動

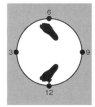 　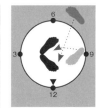　

足の動作／左足を軸に右足を6時方向に引く。体の向きは3時方向。
立ち方／四股立ち。
手の動作／右掌にて左肘の方向へ押さえ受けをする。左拳にて12時方向へ上段裏拳打ちを行い、肩の高さに引く。

Feet: Pull the right foot in the direction of 6 o'clock pivoting on the left foot. The direction of the body is at 3 o'clock.
Stance: Sikodachi.
Hands: Do Osae-uke in the direction of the left elbow with the right hand. Do Jodan Uraken-uchi in the direction of 12 o'clock with left fist and pull the fist to the height of the shoulder.

足の動作／右足を右斜め前に一歩踏み出すと同時に、左足を右足に引き寄せ結び立ちになる。目付は12時方向を向く。
立ち方／結び立ち。
手の動作／右拳は握り甲を下に向け、左手は開手にて指を横にして左掌を右拳の正拳に添える。

Feet: Take the right foot one step to the right diagonally forward. At the same time, draws the left foot to the right foot to Musubidachi stance. The line of sight is at 12 o'clock.
Stance: Musubidachi.
Hands: Put the left palm sideways in front of the right Seiken with its back facing down.

足の動作／そのまま。
立ち方／結び立ち。
手の動作／右拳は体に沿って捻転させながら水月前に置く。手の甲は上に向ける。左掌は右拳に押されるようにして指を上向きに立て水月前。
＊体側まで引かないこと。

Feet: Keep in the same position as ⑰.
Stance: Musubidachi.
Hands: Right fist is placed in front of the solar plexus while twisting along the body. The right fist's back is turned upward. Put the left palm with the finger facing up in front of the solar plexus and press the left palm with the right fist.
＊ Do not pull to the side.

サイファ

移行動作（9時方向から） 裏打ちしたところ 9 挙動

⑲

⑳

㉑

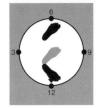

足の動作／右足を軸に左足を6時方向に引く。体の向きは9時方向。
立ち方／四股立ち。
手の動作／左掌にて右肘の方向へ押さえ受けをする。右拳にて12時方向へ上段裏拳打ちを行い、肩の高さに引く。

Transition Movement
(view from 9 o'clock)

Uraken-uchi

Feet: Pull the left foot in the direction of 6 o'clock with pivoting on the right foot. The direction of the body is at 9 o'clock.
Stance: Sikodachi.
Hands: Do Osae-uke in the direction of the right elbow with the left hand. Do Jodan Uraken-uchi in the direction of 12 o'clock with right fist and pull the fist to the height of the shoulder.

● 挙動の分解　Kumite in detail

10 挙動　　　　11 挙動　　　　12 挙動

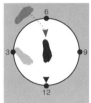
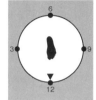
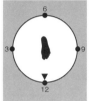

足の動作／左足を一歩、右足の横に平行に移動する。右足を上げて足裏を床と平行にし、上足底を反らせて正面に向ける。目付けと体の向きは12時の方向。
立ち方／左鷺足立ち。
手の動作／開手にて左手掬い受け、右手は側方に押さえ受けをする。

Feet: Bring the left foot to the side of the right foot with one step parallel. Raise the right foot and make the sole parallel to the floor and warp the toe to turn the upper sole forward. The line of sight and the direction of the body, in the direction of 12 o'clock.
Stance: Left Sagiashidachi.
Hands: Do Left Kaishu Sukui-uke. Do Osae-uke to the side with the right hand.

足の動作／右足で中段前蹴りを行う。
立ち方／左鷺足立ち。
手の動作／そのまま。

Feet: Do Right Chudan Mae-geri with the right foot.
Stance: Left Sagiashidachi.
Hands: Keep in the same position as ㉒.

足の動作／右足を引く。
立ち方／左鷺足立ち。
手の動作／そのまま。

Feet: Pull back the kicked right foot.
Stance: Left Sagiashidachi.
Hands: Keep in the same position as ㉒.

サイファ

相手の右中段突きを左手で掬い受け。

Block your opponent's Right Chudan Zuki with a Sukui-uke using your left hand.

さらに左中段突に対して押さえ受けを行う。

Block your opponent's Left Chudan Zuki with an Osae-uke.

右中段前蹴りを行う。

Perform a Right Chudan Mae-geri.

13 挙動 　　　14 挙動 　　　15 挙動

㉕

㉖

㉗

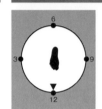

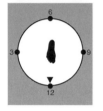

足の動作／蹴った右足は左足横線上に大きく一歩開いて足を下ろす。左足を上げて足裏を床と平行にし、上足底を反らせて正面に向ける。目付けと体の向きは 12 時の方向。
立ち方／右鷺足立ち。
手の動作／開手にて右手掬い受け、左手は側方に押さえ受けをする。

Feet: Open the kicked right foot a lot and parallel to the left foot and lower it. Raise the left foot and make the sole parallel to the floor and warp the toe to turn the upper sole forward. The line of sight and the direction of the body, in the direction of 12 o'clock.
Stance: Right Sagiashidachi.
Hands: Do Right Kaishu Sukui-uke. Do Osae-uke to the side with the left hand.

足の動作／左足で中段前蹴りを行う。
立ち方／右鷺足立ち。
手の動作／そのまま。

Feet: Do Left Chudan Mae-geri with the left foot.
Stance: Right Sagiashidachi.
Hands: Keep in the same position as ㉕.

足の動作／左足を引く。
立ち方／右鷺足立ち。
手の動作／そのまま。

Feet: Pull back the kicked left foot.
Stance: Right Sagiashidachi.
Hands: Keep in the same position as ㉕.

●挙動の分解　Kumite in detail

移行動作　　　　　　途中動作　　　　　　途中動作

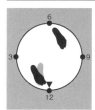

足の動作／蹴った左足を大きく引いて、右前屈立ちになる。
立ち方／右前屈立ち。
手の動作／開手にて両手を交差させる。

Feet: Pull the kicked left foot a lot and take to Right Zenkutsudachi stance.
Stance: Right Zenkutsudachi.
Hands: Cross the both arms with the Kaishu.

足の動作／そのまま
立ち方／右前屈立ち。
手の動作／両開手を前方に伸ばす。

Feet: Keep in the same position as ㉘.
Stance: Right Zenkutsudachi.
Hands: Extend both arms forward with hands open.

足の動作／そのまま。
立ち方／右前屈立ち。
手の動作／両手は内側から円を描くようにして引きながら握る。

Feet: Keep in the same position as ㉘.
Stance: Right Zenkutsudachi.
Hands: Move both hands from the inside to the outside as if drew a circle and make fists while pulling both hands back.

サイファ

16 挙動　　17 挙動　　18 挙動

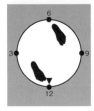
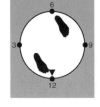

足の動作／そのまま。
立ち方／右前屈立ち。
手の動作／そのままの姿勢（握拳）で両拳を脇に引く。両手の甲は上に向ける。

Feet: Keep in the same position as ㉚.
Stance: Right Zenkutsudachi.
Hands: Pull both fists aside with the same posture (fist). The backs of both hands face upward.

足の動作／そのまま。
立ち方／右前屈立ち。
手の動作／中段の双手突きを行う。両手の甲は上に向ける。

Feet: Keep in the same position as ㉚.
Stance: Right Zenkutsudachi.
Hands: Do Chudan Morote-zuki. Take the back of both hands face up.

足の動作／そのまま
立ち方／右前屈立ち。
手の動作／双手突きをした腕を伸ばしたまま両拳を左右に大きく円を描きながら上体を前に傾けて左拳を開き、右拳槌にて前方下方部の左掌を打つ。
＊目付は下方前方を見る。

Feet: Keep in the same position as ㉚.
Stance: Right Zenkutsudachi.
Hands: Incline the upper body forward while drawing a large circle on both sides with both fists while extending arms, and hit the left palm of the lower front part with the right Kentsui.
＊ The line of sight looks front downward.

●挙動の分解　Kumite in detail

相手が両肩を掴んでくる。

Your opponent grabs both of your shoulders.

相手の両手の内側より両手を差し込み

Insert both of your arms between your opponent's arms.

両手の手をはずす。

Release both hands.

すかさず双手突きを行う。

Immediately perform a Morote-zuki.

116

移行動作（9時方向から）   19 挙動   移行動作

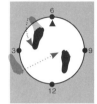

足の動作／左足を軸にして右足を左足の前を交差させ、左廻りに6時方向に向き、左三戦立ちとなる。
立ち方／左三戦立ち。
手の動作／左手は掛け手、右手は開手で水月前に構える。

足の動作／左足を6時方向に運ぶ。
立ち方／左前屈立ち。
手の動作／開手にて両手を交差させる。

Transition Movement
(view from 9 o'clock)

Feet: Cross the right foot to the front of the left foot with pivoting on the left foot. Turns counterclockwise to the direction of 6 o'clock, and take Sanchindachi stance.
Stance: Left Sanchindachi.
Hands: Do Kakete with left hand and hold the right hand in front of the solar plexus.

Feet: Bring the left foot 6 o'clock direction.
Stance: Left Zenkutsudachi.
Hands: Cross the both arms with the Kaishu.

サイファ

相手が前足の内膝と外足首を押さえて倒そうとしてくる。

すかさず相手の両耳を左掌と右拳で打つ。

Your opponent tries to knock you down by pushing on the back of the knee of your front leg and the outer side of your ankle.

Immediately strike both of your opponent's ears with your left palm and right fist.

途中動作（6時方向から）	20 挙動	21 挙動

足の動作／そのまま。
立ち方／左前屈立ち。
手の動作／両開手を前方に伸ばす。

Feet: Keep in the same position as ㊱.
Stance: Left Zenkutsudachi.
Hands: Extend both hands forward.

足の動作／そのまま。
立ち方／左前屈立ち。
手の動作／左拳を握って脇に引く。手の甲は上に向ける。

Feet: Keep in the same position as ㊱.
Stance: Left Zenkutsudachi.
Hands: Pull both fists aside to the armpits. The backs of both hands face upward.

足の動作／そのまま。
立ち方／左前屈立ち。
手の動作／中段の双手突きを行う。両手の甲は上に向ける。

Feet: Keep in the same position as ㊱.
Stance: Left Zenkutsudachi.
Hands: Do Chudan Morote-zuki. The backs of both hands face upward.

●挙動の分解　Kumite in detail

22挙動〜30挙動

相手が後方から肩を掴もうとした瞬間。
Your opponent is about to grab your shoulder from behind.

回り込み左手で打ち落とす。
Spin around and knock down his arm with your left hand.

左足で相手の右足を払う。
Sweep away your opponent's right leg with your left leg.

相手の右手を巻き込みながら投げる。
While clinching up your opponent's right hand, throw him.

22 挙動　　　移行動作　　　23 挙動

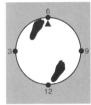     

足の動作／そのまま
立ち方／左前屈立ち。
手の動作／双手突きをした腕を伸ばしたまま両拳を左右に大きく円を描きながら上体を前に傾け、左拳槌にて前方下方部の右掌を打つ。
＊この時目付は下方前方を見る。

Feet: Keep in the same position as ㊴
Stance: Left Zenkutsudachi.
Hands: Tilt the upper body forward while drawing a large circle on both sides with both fists while extending arms,and hit the right palm of the lower front part with the left Kentsui.
＊ At this time the line of sight looks front downward.

足の動作／左足を軸に後方（12時方向）に向きながら右足を大きく跳ね上げ、足払いを行う。
手の動作／右拳を左肩の方へ。左拳は左脇に引く。

Feet: Raise your right foot greatly while turning backward (direction of 12 o'clock) pivoting on the left foot, and do Ashibarai.
Hands: Right fist toward the left shoulder. Pull the left fist to the left armpit.

足の動作／跳ね上げた右足を一歩強く踏み出して基立ちとなる。腰は回転させず半身のまま。
立ち方／基立ち。
手の動作／右拳槌にて上段を打つ。左拳は左脇に引く。

Feet: Step strongly on the right foot that was raised up and take the Motodachi stance. Leave the Hanmi without twisting the hips.
Stance: Right Motodachi.
Hands: Hit the Jodan with a right Kentsui.Pull the left fist to the left armpit.

サイファ

倒れた相手を突きで極める。

Finish your fallen opponent with a Tsuki (punch.)

119

24 挙動　　25 挙動　　移行動作

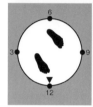 　　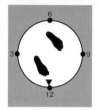　　

足の動作／そのまま。
立ち方／基立ち。
手の動作／右拳を掛け手にする。

Feet: Keep in the same position as ㊷.
Stance: Right Motodachi.
Hands: Change the right fist to Kakete.

足の動作／そのまま。
立ち方／基立ち。
手の動作／右掛け手を開手のまま右脇に引きながら左拳で中段裏突きを行う。

Feet: Keep in the same position as ㊷.
Stance: Right Motodachi.
Hands: Pull right Kakete to the right armpit, at the same time do Chudan Ura-zuki with left fist.

足の動作／右足を軸に後方（6時方向）に向きながら左足を大きく跳ね上げ、足払いを行う。
手の動作／左拳を右肩の方へ。右拳は右脇に引く。

Feet: Raise the left foot greatly while turning backward (direction of 6 o'clock) pivoting on the right foot, and do Ashibarai.
Hands: Left fist toward the right shoulder. Pull the right fist to the right armpit.

●挙動の分解　Kumite in detail

26 挙動

足の動作／跳ね上げた左足を一歩強く踏み出して基立ちとなる。腰は回転させず半身のまま。
立ち方／基立ち。
手の動作／左拳槌にて上段を打つ。右拳は右脇に引く。

Feet: Step strongly on the left foot that was raised up and take the Motodachi stance. Leave the Hanmi without twisting the hips.
Stance: Left Motodachi.
Hands: Hit the Jodan with a left Kentsui. Pull the right fist to the right armpit.

27 挙動

足の動作／そのまま。
立ち方／基立ち。
手の動作／左拳を掛け手にする。

Feet: Keep in the same position as ㊻.
Stance: Left Motodachi.
Hands: Change the left fist to Kakete.

28 挙動

足の動作／そのまま。
立ち方／基立ち。
手の動作／左掛け手を開手のまま左脇に引きながら右拳で中段裏突きを行う。

Feet: Keep in the same position as ㊻.
Stance: Left Motodachi.
Hands: Pull left Kakete to the left armpits, at the same time do Chudan Ura-zuki with right fist.

サイファ

29 挙動

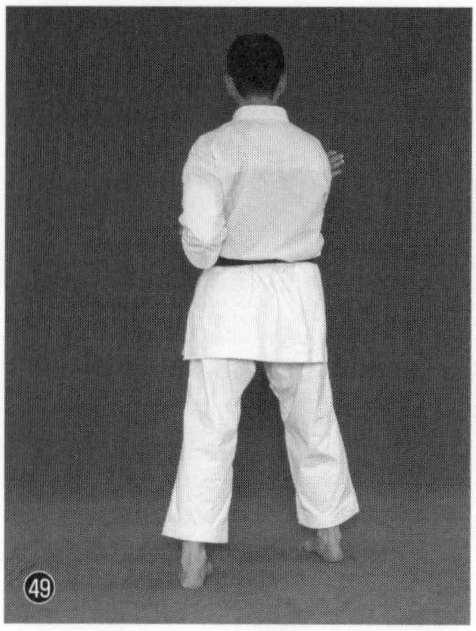

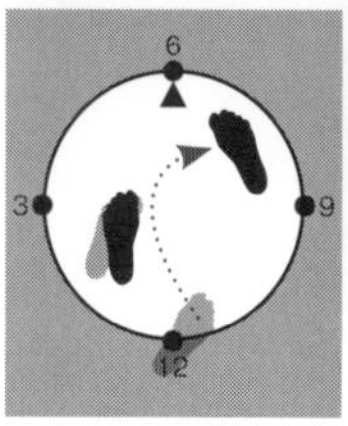

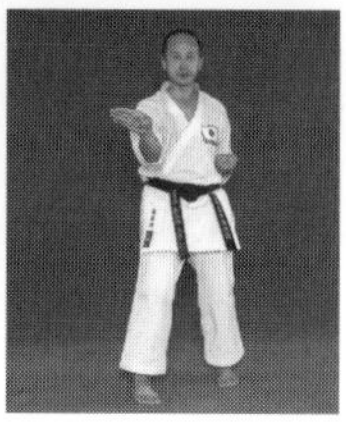

足の動作／左足を軸に右足を一歩出して、右三戦立ちとなる。
立ち方／右三戦立ち。
手の動作／右掛け手、左拳は握って左脇に構える。

Feet: Step forward the right foot to Right Sanchindachi pivoting on the left foot.
Stance: Right Sanchindachi.
Hands: Do Right Kakete and hold the left fist at the left armpit

30 挙動

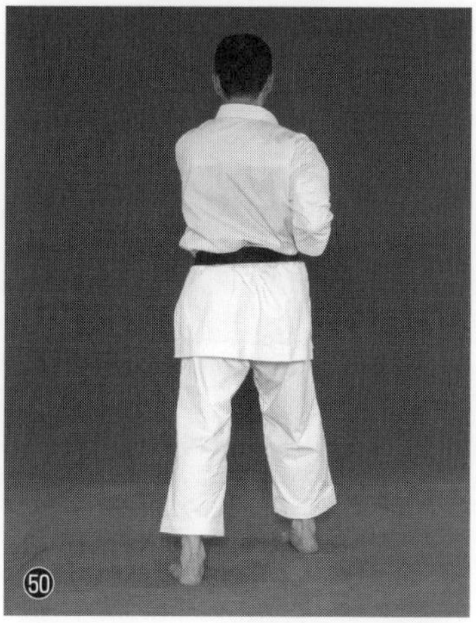

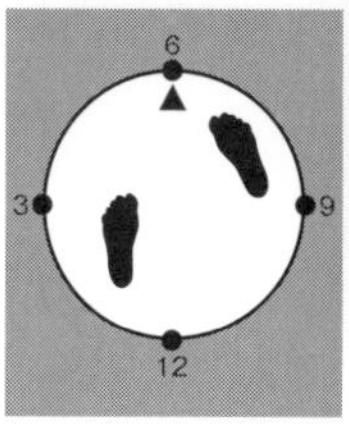

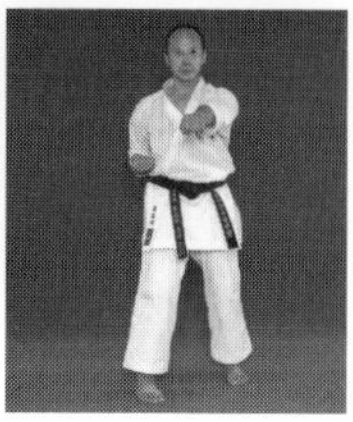

足の動作／そのまま。
立ち方／右三戦立ち。
手の動作／右掛け手を握って右脇に引く。同時に左拳にて中段逆突きを行う。

Feet: Keep in the same position as ㊾ .
Stance: Right Sanchindachi.
Hands: Pull right hand in fist to the right armpit, at the same time do Chudan Gyaku-zuki with left fist.

移行動作

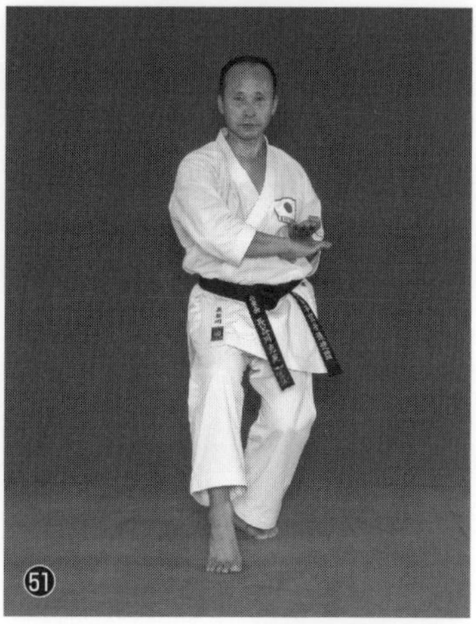

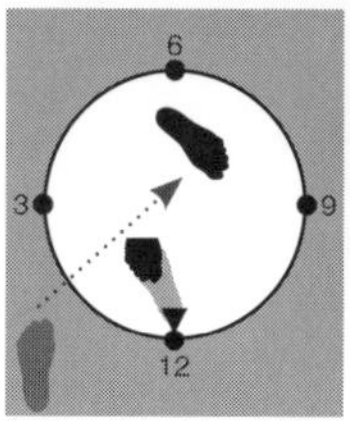

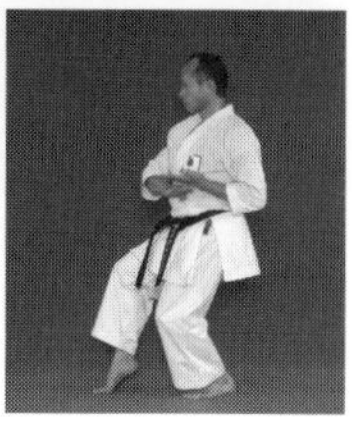

足の動作／右足を軸に左足を右斜め前に出し右回りで、12 時方向を向く。
立ち方／右猫足立ち。
手の動作／左右開手にて左脇構えにする。左手の甲を下に、右手は甲を上に向け、甲を合わせる。

Feet: Blling the left foot obliquely forward right pivotting on right foot and turn clockwise to face the 12 o'clock direction.
Stance: Right Nekoashidachi.
Hands: Do Left Wakigamae with open both hands. Put the back of the left hand facing on the back of the right hand.

●挙動の分解　Kumite in detail

途中動作

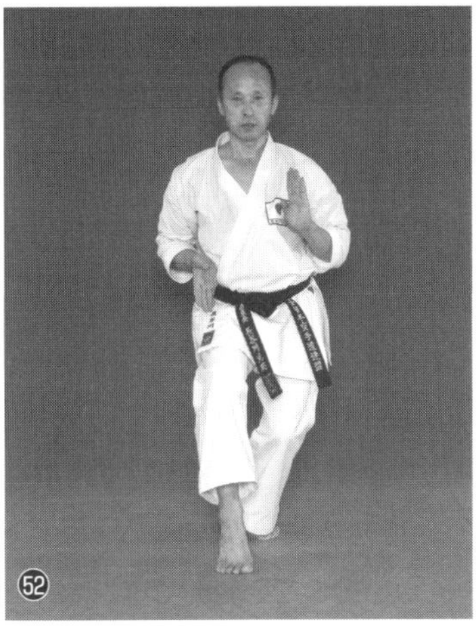

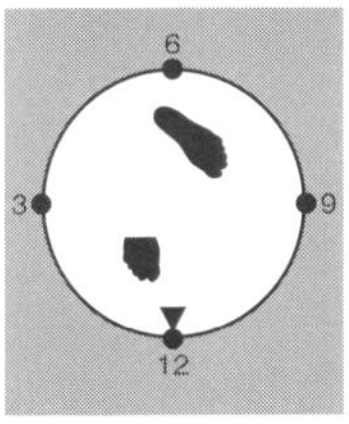

Transition Movement

31 挙動

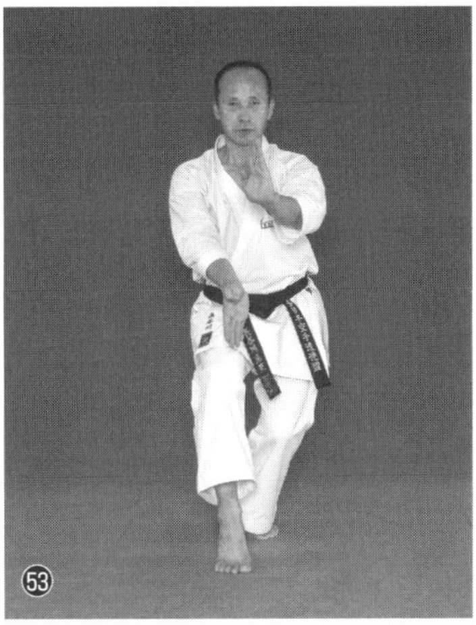

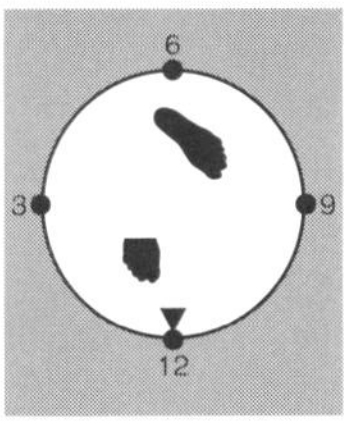

足の動作／そのまま。
立ち方／右猫足立ち。
手の動作／廻し受けを行う。

Feet: Keep in the same position as (51).
Stance: Right Nekoashidachi
Hands: Do Mawashi-uke.

途中動作

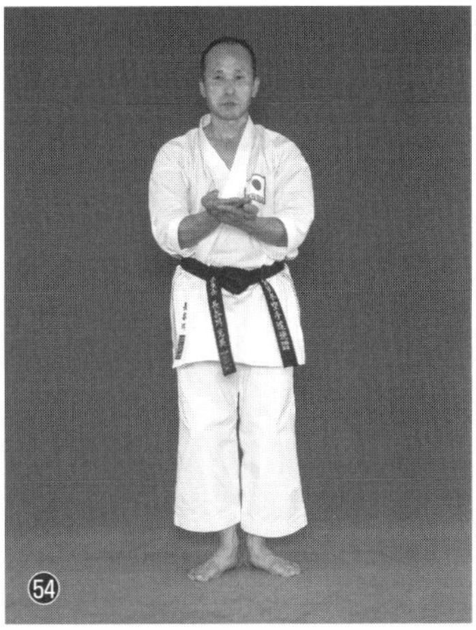

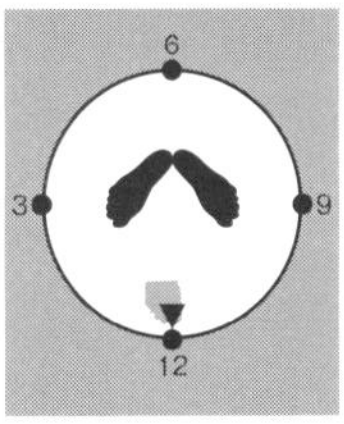

足の動作／右足を左足に引き寄せる。
立ち方／結び立ち。
手の動作／両開手を重ね、水月前に上げる。
＊止めまで連続して行う。

Feet: Pull the right foot to the left foot.
Stance: Musubidachi
Hands: Open both hands and hold them in front of the solar plexus with the right hand putting on the left hand.
＊ Continue to the (55) consecutive.

止め

⑤

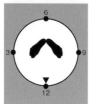

足の動作／そのまま。
立ち方／結び立ち。
手の動作／両手は開手のまま、右甲に左掌を重ねて、床を押さえるように下腹部前に構える。

Feet: Keep in the same position as ⑤.
Stance: Musubidachi.
Hands: Open both hands and hold them in front of the lower abdomen as if pushed down the floor with the left hand putting on the right hand.

気を付けの姿勢

⑤

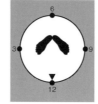

足の動作／そのまま。
立ち方／結び立ち。
手の動作／両開手を大腿部外側へ付ける。

Feet: Keep in the same position as ⑤.
Stance: Musubidachi.
Hands: Stretch both arms with hands putting on both sides of the thighs.

礼

⑤

●挙動の分解　Kumite in detail

気を付けの姿勢

クルルンファ

　クルルンファは、 東恩納系那覇手の形で、 十七とも呼ばれる。

　接近戦を想定し、 投げ技、 倒し技、 逆技、 また羽交い締めの外しなど、 様々な技術が集約された非常に内容の濃い形である。

　那覇手の特徴を活かした演武が要求される。

Kururunfa, also called Ju-Shichi, is a Naha-te Kata of Higaonna's system.

Intended for close combat, it is an unusually deep Kata that collects various techniques including throws, throw downs, reverses, and pinioning releases.

It requires training that makes use of the characteristics of Naha-te.

KURURUNFA

クルルンファ 形の流れ

気を付けの姿勢	礼	直立	途中動作	用意	1 挙動
 ①	 ②	 ③	 ④	 ⑤	 ⑥

途中動作	6 挙動	途中動作	7 挙動	8 挙動	9 挙動
 ⑬	 ⑭	 ⑮	 ⑯	 ⑰	 ⑱

16 挙動	17 挙動	上げ突きしたところ	18 挙動	19 挙動	20 挙動
 ㉕	 ㉖	 ㉗	 ㉘	 ㉙	 ㉚

26 挙動	27 挙動	途中動作	28 挙動	29 挙動	30 挙動
 ㊲	 ㊳	 ㊴	 ㊵	 ㊶	㊷

クルルンファ

35 挙動

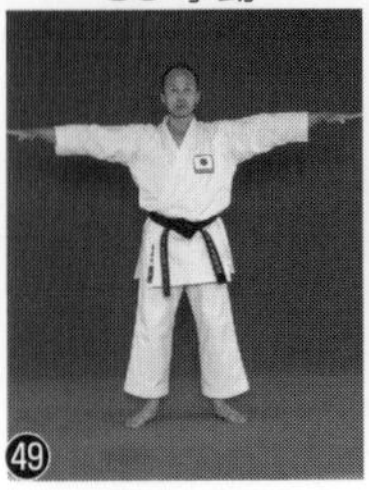

36 挙動

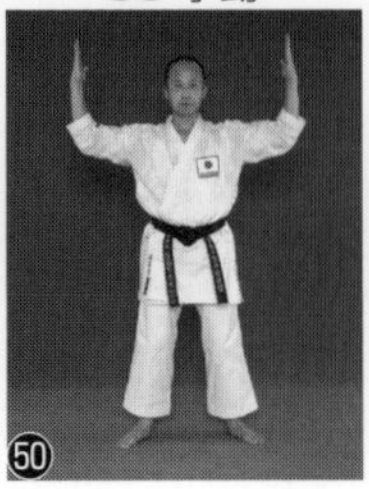

37 挙動

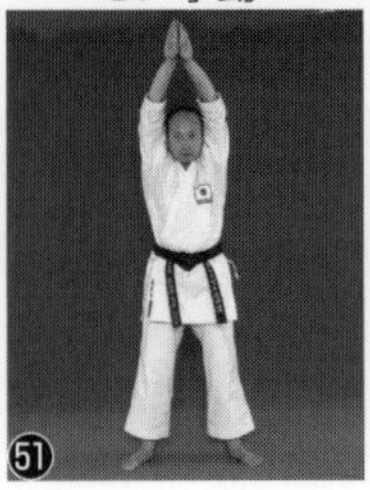

途中動作

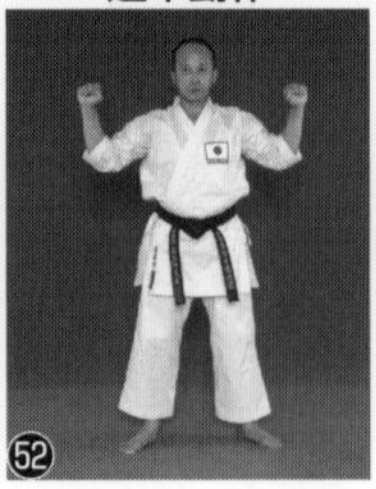

38 挙動

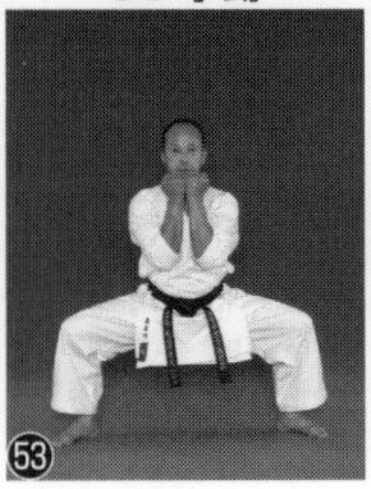

39 挙動

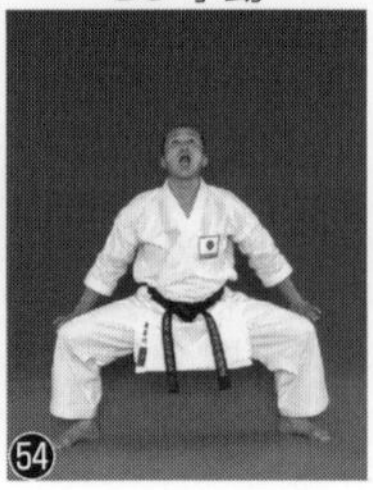

46 挙動

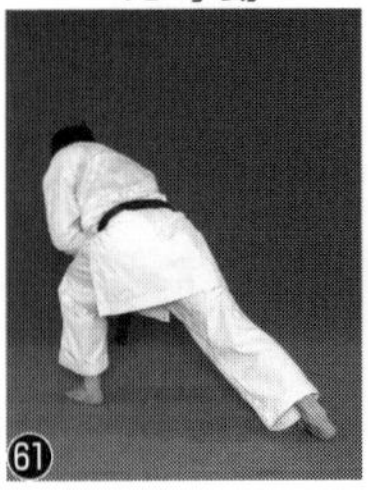

47 挙動

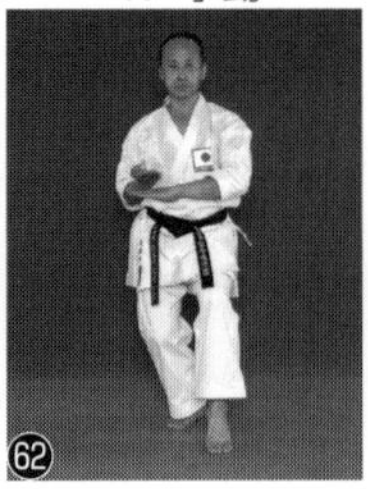

途中動作

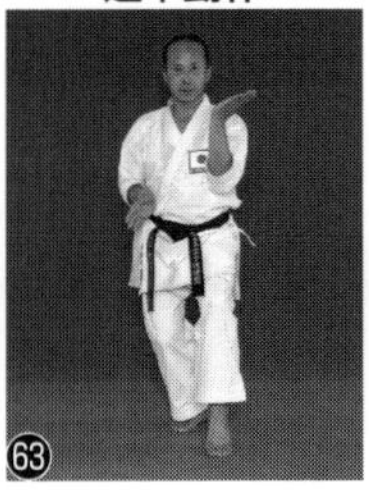

48 挙動

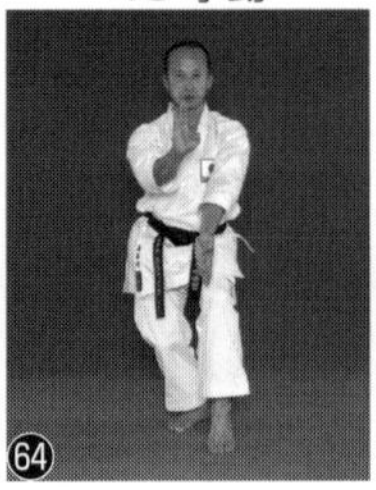

途中動作

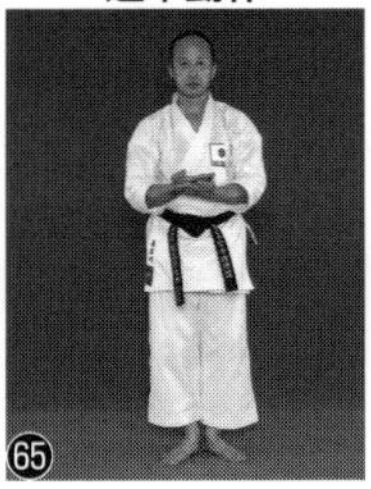

49 挙動

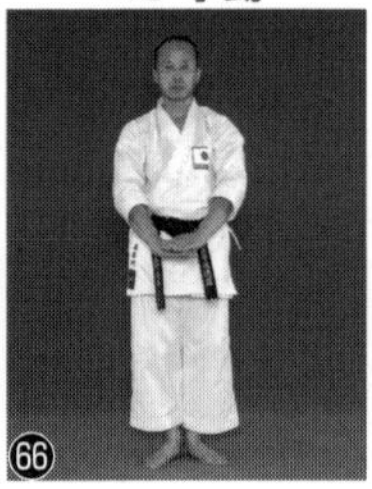

クルルンファ

気を付けの姿勢　　礼　　直立

① ② ③

立ち方／結び立ち。
手の動作／両手を伸ばし、大腿部外側
に付ける。

Stance: Musubidachi
Hands: Stretch both arms with hands
putting on both sides of the thighs.

●挙動の分解　Kumite in detail

途中動作	用意	1 挙動

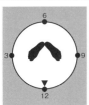	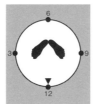	

立ち方／結び立ち。
手の動作／両掌を重ね水月前に上げる。

Stance: Musubidachi.

Hands: Put both hands together and hold them in front of the solar plexus.

立ち方／結び立ち。
手の動作／両手は開手のまま、右甲に左掌を重ねて、床を押すように下腹部前に構える。

Stance: Musubidachi.
Hands: Put the left open hand on the back of the open right hand, and hold them in front of the lower abdomen as if pushed down the floor.

足の動作／右足を3時の方向に引く。
立ち方／左猫足立ち。
手の動作／左袖下を払うように右手刀払い。左手は右肩方向へ引く。

Feet: Pull the right foot in the direction of 3 o'clock.
Stance: Left Nekoashidachi.
Hands: Do Right Shuto-barai as if cutting the bottom of the left sleeve. Pull up the left hand toward the right shoulder.

クルルンファ

2 挙動　　　　途中動作　　　　3 挙動

⑦

⑧

⑨

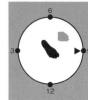

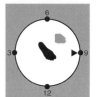

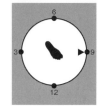

足の動作／そのまま。
立ち方／左猫足立ち。
手の動作／左中段手刀受け。
右手は開手で甲を下にして水月前に引く。

Feet: Keep in the same position as ❻.
Stance: Left Nekoashidachi.
Hands: Do Left Chudan Shuto-uke. Pull the right open hand in front of the solar plexus with back of the hand down.

足の動作／右足は元位置。左膝を高く引き上げる。
＊足刀部を膝の高さまで上げる。
手の動作／そのまま。

Feet: Pull up the left knee high. Right foot is same position as ❼.
＊ Raise the part of Sokuto to the knee height.
Hands: Keep in the same position as ❼.

足の動作／左下段足刀蹴り。右足は元位置。
手の動作／そのまま。

Feet: Do Left Gedan Sokuto-geri. Right foot is same position as ❼.
Hands: Keep in the same position as ❼.

●挙動の分解　Kumite in detail

1挙動〜6挙動

相手が自分の左袖を取り攻撃をしようとする。

Your opponent grabs your left sleeve and tries to attack.

右斜め後方へ転身しながら取ってくる相手の手首を手刀で打ち払う。これと同時に左手を右肩のあたりに引く。

While shifting your body backwards to the right, sweep aside your attacking opponent's wrist with a Shuto strike. At the same time, draw your left hand to your right shoulder.

さらに相手の左中段突きに対して、左手刀受け。

Block your opponent's Left Chudan Zuki with a Left Shuto-uke.

途中動作	4 挙動	5 挙動

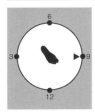	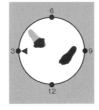	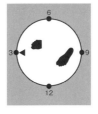

足の動作／左膝を高く引き上げる。右足は元位置。
手の動作／そのまま。

Feet: Pull up the left knee high. Right foot is same position as ❼.
Hands: Keep in the same position as ❼.

足の動作／左足を9時方向に移動して下ろす。
立ち方／右猫足立ち。
手の動作／右袖下を払うように左手刀払い。右手は左肩方向へ引く。

Feet: Bring the left foot in the direction of 9 o'clock and lower it.
Stance: Right Nekoashidachi.
Hands: Do Left Shuto-barai as if cutting off the bottom of the right sleeve. Pull up the right hand toward the left shoulder.

足の動作／そのまま。
立ち方／猫足立ち。
手の動作／右中段手刀受け。

Feet: Keep in the same position as ⑪.
Stance: Right Nekoashidachi.
Hands: Do Right Chudan Shuto-uke.

左手刀受けと同時に相手の腕をつかみ、左足刀で右膝内側に蹴り込む。

手を引きながら裏突き。

(裏突きでの極めを反対側から見たところ)

At the same time as the Left Shuto-uke, grab your opponent's arm and kick the inside of his right knee with a Left Sokuto.

While pulling his hand, do an Ura-zuki.

(the view of the Ura-zuki from the other side)

クルルンファ

途中動作	6 挙動	途中動作

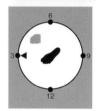		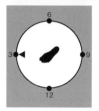

足の動作／右膝を高く引き上げる。左足は元位置。
＊足刀部を膝の高さまで上げる。
手の動作／そのまま。

Feet: Pull up the right knee high. Left foot is same position as ⑫.
＊ Raise the part of Sokuto to the knee height.
Hands: Keep in the same position as ⑫.

足の動作／右下段足刀蹴り。左足は元位置。
手の動作／そのまま。

Feet: Do Right Gedan Sokuto-geri. Left foot is same position as ⑫.
Hands: Keep in the same position as ⑫.

足の動作／右膝を高く引き上げる。左足は元位置。
手の動作／そのまま。

Feet: Pull up the right knee high. Left foot is same position as ⑫.
Hands: Keep in the same position as ⑫.

●挙動の分解　Kumite in detail

7 挙動	8 挙動	9 挙動

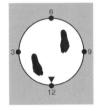	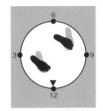	

足の動作／12時の方向を向き、蹴った右足を下ろす。
立ち方／右三戦立ち。
手の動作／右中段掬い受け、左開手下段払いをゆっくり行う。

Feet: Turn the body in the direction of 12 o'clock and lower the right foot.
Stance: Right Sanchindachi.
Hands: Do Right Chudan Sukui-uke. Left Kaishu Gedan Barai slowly.

足の動作／早い動作で上足底を軸に腰を回す。この時、上体は反る。
立ち方／狭い後屈立ち。
手の動作／右開手下段払い。左開手は甲を下に水月前に構える。

Feet: Turn the hips pivoting on the both upper soles with an quick action. At this time, the upper body warps.
Stance: Narrow Koukutsudachi.
Hands: Do Right Kaishu Gedan Barai. Hold the left open hand in front of the solar plexus with back of the hand down.

足の動作／上足底を軸に⑯の姿勢に戻る。
立ち方／右三戦立ち。
手の動作／右中段掬い受けと左開手下段払いをゆっくり同時に行う。

Feet: Turn to the ⑯ posture pivoting on the both upper soles.
Stance: Right Sanchindachi.
Hands: Do Right Chudan Sukui-uke and Left Kaisyu Gedan Barai slowly at the same time.

クルルンファ

7挙動～15挙動

相手の右中段追い突きに対して、右斜め後方に転身し、左手を開き中段払い受け。
Block your opponent's Right Chudan Oi-zuki by shifting your body backwards to the right, then opening your left hand and doing a Chudan Harai-uke.

相手の左中段突きを右手で掬い受けを行う。
Block your opponent's Left Chudan Zuki with a Sukui-uke using your right hand.

左中段蹴りに対し、右足を右斜め後方へ引き、後屈立ちに変化する。手を開いて手首を曲げ、掌底に力を入れ円を描くように払い受け。
In response to the Left Chudan Geri, pull your right leg backward to the right, and assume the Kokutsudachi stance. Open your hand, strain your Shotei, and perform a Harai-uke as if drawing a circle.

基立ちとなり相手の側面を右拳にて中段裏突きを行う。
Assume the Motodachi stance and perform a Chudan Ura-zuki on your opponent's side with your right fist.

10 挙動　　　11 挙動　　　12 挙動

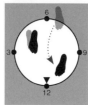

足の動作／左足を前へ運ぶ。
立ち方／左三戦立ち。
手の動作／左中段掬い受けと右下段払いをゆっくり同時に行う。

Feet: Step forward with the left foot.
Stance: Left Sanchindachi.
Hands: Do Left Chudan Sukui-uke and the Right Gedan Barai slowly at the same time.

足の動作／早い動作で上足底を軸に腰を回す。この時、上体は反る。
立ち方／狭い後屈立ち。
手の動作／左開手下段払い。右開手は甲を下に水月前に構える。

Feet:Turn the hips pivoting on the both upper soles with an quick action.At this time, the upper body warps.
Stance: Narrow Right Koukutsudachi.
Hands: Do Left Kaishu Gedan Barai. Hold the Right open hand in front of the solar plexus with back of the hand down.

足の動作／上足底を軸に⑲の姿勢に戻る。
立ち方／三戦立ち。
手の動作／左中段掬い受けと右開手下段払いをゆっくり同時に行う。

Feet: Turn to the ⑲ posture pivoting on the both upper soles.
Stance: Left Sanchindachi.
Hands: Do Left Chudan Sukui-uke and Right Kaisyu Gedan Barai slowly at the same time.

●挙動の分解　Kumite in detail

13 挙動　　　　　14 挙動　　　　　15 挙動

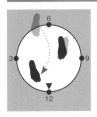
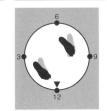
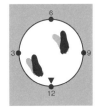

足の動作／右足を前へ運ぶ。
立ち方／三戦立ち。
手の動作／右掬い受けと左下段払いをゆっくり同時に行う。

Feet: Step forward with the right foot.
Stance: Right Sanchindachi.
Hands: Do Right Chudan Sukui-uke and the Left Gedan Barai slowly at the same time.

足の動作／早い動作で上足底を軸に腰を回す。この時、上体は反る。
立ち方／狭い後屈立ち。
手の動作／右開手下段払い。左開手は甲を下に水月前に構える。

Feet: Turn the hips pivoting on the both upper soles with an quick action.
Stance: Narrow Left Koukutsudachi.
Hands: Do Right Kaishu Gedan Barai. Hold the Left open hand in front of the solar plexus with back of the hand down.

足の動作／上足底を軸に㉒の姿勢に戻る。
立ち方／三戦立ち。
手の動作／右中段掬い受けと左開手下段払いをゆっくり同時に行う。

Feet: Turn to the ㉒ posture pivoting on the both upper soles.
Stance: Right Sanchindachi.
Hands: Do Right Chudan Sukui-uke and Left Kaisyu Gedan Barai slowly at the same time.

クルルンファ

16 挙動　　17 挙動　　上げ突きしたところ

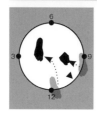

足の動作／右足を斜め後ろに下げる。
立ち方／左猫足立ち。
手の動作／左中段裏受け、右手は手首を立て水月前に構える（ゆっくり行う）。

Feet: Pull the right foot obliquely backward.
Stance: Left Nekoashidachi.
Hands: Do Left Chudan Ura-uke. Hold the right hand standing vertically in front of the solar plexus. (do it slowly)

足の動作／そのまま。
立ち方／左猫足立ち。
手の動作／右手を前に押さえる（ゆっくり行う）。

Feet: Keep in the same position as ㉕.
Stance: Left Nekoashidachi.
Hands: Push right hand forward. (do it slowly)

足の動作／寄り足を行う。
立ち方／左猫足立ち。
手の動作／左上段上げ突き。

Feet: Step forward (Yoriashi).
Stance: Left Nekoashidachi.
Hands: Do Left Jodan Age-zuki.

●挙動の分解　Kumite in detail

相手の右中段突きに対し、左足を左斜め後方へ引き、猫足立ちとなって右手で裏受けをする。左手は開いて水月の前に構える。

Block your opponent's Right Chudan Zuki by pulling your left leg back to the left, assuming the Nekoashidachi stance, and do Ura-uke with your right hand. Hold the left open hand in front of the solar plexus.

左手で相手の腕を押さえる。

Seize your opponent's arm with your left hand.

寄り足にて踏み込み、右拳で揚げ突きをする。

Step forward with a sliding step (Yoriashi) and perform an Age-zuki with your right fist.

右揚げ突きを相手が右足を一歩引いて左小手で上から払い受けでかわす。

Your opponent dodges the Right Age-zuki by pulling his right leg back one step and performing a Harai-uke from above with his left forearm.

140

18 挙動

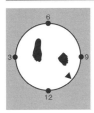

足の動作／そのまま。
立ち方／左猫足立ち。
手の動作／突いた左手は直ちに肩の高さへ引き戻す。

Feet: Keep in the same position as ㉗.
Stance: Left Nekoashidachi.
Hands: Pull back the left fist immediately to the height of the shoulder.

19 挙動

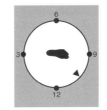

足の動作／右中段前蹴り。
手の動作／そのまま。

Feet: Do Right Chudan Mae-geri.
Hands: Keep in the same position as ㉘.

20 挙動

足の動作／蹴った右足を下ろす。
立ち方／四股立ち。
手の動作／右中段肘当て（肘当ては肩の高さ）。左手は指を立て、水月前に引く。

Feet: Lower the kicked right foot.
Stance: Shikodachi.
Hands: Do Right Chudan Hiji-ate (to shoulder height). Hold the left hand standing vertically and pull back in front of the solar plexus.

相手の払い受けの腕の手首を直ちに掴む。
Immediately seize the wrist of your opponent's Harai-uke arm.

相手の手首を掴むと同時にこれを引きながら左中段蹴りを行う。
At the same time as seizing your opponent's wrist, while pulling this, perform a Left Chudan Geri.

蹴った足を踏み込むと同時に左肘当てを行う。
Step forward with the leg that you kicked and perform a Left Hiji-ate at the same time.

体制を低く前屈立ちとなり、右手で相手の足首を取り、左掌底にて膝関節部を内側より押す。
Keep your body low and assume the Zenkutsudachi stance. Seize your opponent's ankle with your right hand and push on the inside of the knee joint area with your Left Shotei.

クルルンファ

21 挙動　　　　22 挙動　　　　23 挙動

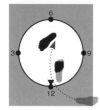
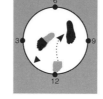
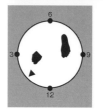

足の動作／右足を引き、12時方向に猫足立ち。
立ち方／左猫足立ち。
手の動作／左手甲を上に、右手甲を下に水月前に構える。

Feet: Pull the right foot and turn the body in the direction of 12 o'clock. take Nekoashidachi stance.
Stance: Leftt Nekoashidachi.
Hands: Hold the left hand up and the right hand down, so that the palms face each other and set up in front of the solar plexus.

足の動作／左足を斜め後ろに引く。
立ち方／右猫足立ち。
手の動作／右中段裏受け、左手は手首を立て、水月前に構える（ゆっくり行う）。

Feet: Pull the left foot obliquely backward.
Stance: Right Nekoashidachi.
Hands: Do Right Chudan Ura-uke. Hold the left hand standing vertically in front of the solar plexus. (do it slowly)

足の動作／そのまま。
立ち方／右猫足立ち。
手の動作／左手を前に押さえる（ゆっくり行う）。

Feet: Keep in the same position as ㉜.
Stance: Right Nekoashidachi.
Hands: Push left hand forward. (do it slowly)

●挙動の分解　Kumite in detail

右手で足首を掴んで引いて倒す。
Grab your opponent's ankle with your right hand and pull it to knock him down.

足刀蹴りで極める。
Finish with a Sokutou-geri.

142

上げ突きしたところ	24 挙動	25 挙動

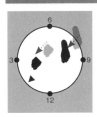	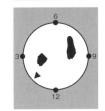	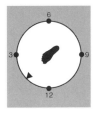

足の動作／寄り足を行う。
立ち方／右猫足立ち。
手の動作／右上段上げ突き。

Feet: Step forward.(Yoriashi)
Stance: Right Nekoashidachi.
Hands: Do Right Jodan Age-zuki.

足の動作／そのまま。
立ち方／右猫足立ち。
手の動作／突いた右手は直ちに肩の高さへ引き戻す。

Feet: Keep in the same position as ㉞.
Stance: Right Nekoashidachi.
Hands: Pull back the right fist immediately to the height of the shoulder.

足の動作／左中段前蹴り。
手の動作／そのまま。

Feet: Do Left Chudan Mae-geri.
Hands: Keep in the same position as ㉟.

クルルンファ

26 挙動　　27 挙動　　途中動作

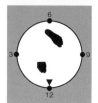

足の動作／蹴った左足を踏み出す。
立ち方／四股立ち。
手の動作／左中段肘当て（肘当ては肩の高さ）。右手は指を立て、水月前に引く。

Feet: Step forward the kicked left foot.
Stance: Shikodachi.
Hands: Do Left Chudan Hiji-ate(to shoulder height).Hold the right hand standing vertically and pull back in front of the solar plexus.

足の動作／左足を引き、12時方向に猫足立ち。
立ち方／右猫足立ち。
手の動作／右手甲を上に、左手甲を下に水月前に構える。

Feet: Pull the left foot and turn the body in the direction of 12 o'clock. Take Nekoashidachi stance.
Stance: Right Nekoashidachi.
Hands: Hold the right hand up and the left hand down, so that the palms face each other and set up in front of the solar plexus.

Transition Movement

●挙動の分解　Kumite in detail

相手の右中段前蹴りに対し、右足を後方に引いて体を捌き、両手で踵及び爪先を取る。
In response to your opponent's Right Chudan Mae-geri, pull your right leg back and deflect your body away from the attack, and then seize your opponent's heel and toes with both hands.

掴んだ相手の足を回す。
Twist your opponent's seized leg.

相手の足を引き付けて倒す。
Pull your opponent's leg towards you to knock him down.

自分の右足を相手の足に挟む。
Insert your right leg in his leg.

28 挙動   29 挙動   30 挙動

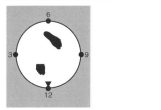
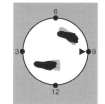
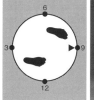

足の動作／そのまま。
立ち方／右猫足立ち。
手の動作／両手を小さく回す（相手の足を捻るため）。

Feet: Keep in the same position as ㊳.
Stance: Right Nekoashidachi.
Hands: Rotate both hands small (to twist the opponent's leg).

足の動作／上足底を軸に9時の方向へ向く。
立ち方／左三戦立ち。
手の動作／左手で開手中段横受け。右手は指先を左肘に添える。

Feet: Turn the body in the direction of 9 o'clock, pivoting on the upper soles.
Stance: Left Sanchindachi.
Hands: Do Left kaisyu Chudan Yoko-uke. Put the fingertips of the right hand on the side of the left elbow.

足の動作／そのまま。
立ち方／左三戦立ち。
手の動作／左掛け手を行う。右手はそのまま。

Feet: Keep in the same position as ㊶.
Stance: Left Sanchindachi.
Hands: Do Left Kakete. Right hand as it is.

手を離し相手の帯をつかみ前傾し、自分の体重を相手の足先にかけて極める。

Release your hands, seize your opponent's Obi (belt), and lean your body weight on your opponent's toes to finish.

クルルンファ

移行動作	31 挙動	32 挙動

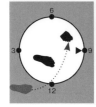	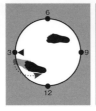	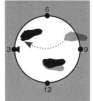

足の動作／右足を左方に移動させ、上足底を着ける。
手の動作／そのまま。

Feet: Bring the right foot to the left and put the upper sole.
Hands: Keep in the same position as ㊷.

足の動作／上足底を軸に3時方向に反転する。
立ち方／左三戦立ち。
手の動作／右肘当て、左手は同時に前へ押し出す。

Feet: Turn the body counterclockwise pivoting on the upper soles in the direction of 3 o'clock.
Stance: Left Sanchindachi.
Hands: Do Right Hiji-ate. Push left hand forward at the same time.

足の動作／右足を3時方向に運ぶ。
立ち方／右三戦立ち。
手の動作／右手で開手中段横受け。
左手は指先を右肘に添える。

Feet: Bring the right foot in the direction of 3 o'clock.
Stance: Right Sanchindachi.
Hands: Do Right kaishu Chudan Yoko-uke. Put the fingertips of the left hand on the side of the right elbow.

●挙動の分解　Kumite in detail

相手の右中段突きに対し、左後方へ転身し、右開手中段横受け。

Block your opponent's Right Chudan Zuki by shifting your body to the rear left and performing a Right Kaishu Chudan Yoko-uke.

相手の手首を握る。

Seize your opponent's wrist.

手首を握ったまま踏み込んで向きを変え相手の腕を引き肘当て。

While holding your opponent's wrist, step forward, change directions, pull your opponent's arm and perform a Hiji-ate.

相手の手首を掴み、左手にて手の甲を取り、右手を添えて左足を一歩踏み出して腕を上に大きく振りかぶって向きを変える。

Grab your opponent's wrist, take the back of his hand with your left hand, add your right hand, take a step forward with your left foot, raise your arms high above and change directions.

33 挙動　　　移行動作　　　34 挙動

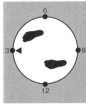    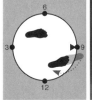 

足の動作／そのまま。
立ち方／右三戦立ち。
手の動作／右掛け手を行う。左手はそのまま。

Feet: Keep in the same position as ㊺.
Stance: Right Sanchindachi.
Hands: Do Right Kakete. Left hand as it is.

足の動作／左足を右方に移動させ、上足底を着ける。
手の動作／そのまま。

Feet: Bring the left foot to the right and put the upper sole.
Hands: Keep in the same position as ㊻.

足の動作／上足底を軸に9時方向に反転する。
立ち方／右三戦立ち。
手の動作／左肘当て、右手は同時に前へ押し出す。

Feet: Turn the body in the direction of 9 o'clock, pivoting on the upper soles.
Stance: Right Sanchindachi.
Hands: Do Left Hiji-ate. The right hand pushes forward at the same time.

相手の腕を逆関節に極めて投げる。　　腰を落として突きを極める。

Lock the joint of your opponent's arm in reverse and throw him down.　　Lower your hips and finish with a Tsuki (punch.)

クルルンファ

35 挙動	36 挙動	37 挙動

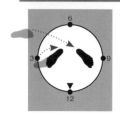	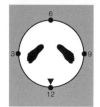	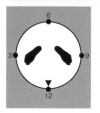

足の動作／左足を9時方向に移動し12時方向を向く。
立ち方／八字立ち。
手の動作／両手は肩の高さで甲を上にして水平に伸ばす（ゆっくり行う）。

Feet: Bring the left foot in the direction of 9 o'clock, and turn the body in the direction of 12 o'clock.
Stance: Hachijidachi.
Hands: Hold both arms horizontally at the shoulder height with the back of the hand up.(do it slowly)

足の動作／そのまま。
立ち方／八字立ち。
手の動作／両手を曲げて手のひらを内側に向ける（ゆっくり行う）。

Feet: Keep in the same position as ㊾.
Stance: Hachijidachi.
Hands: Bend both arms with the palm facing inward. (do it slowly)

足の動作／そのまま。
立ち方／八字立ち。
手の動作／両手の甲を内側に向けて上に伸ばす。

Feet: Keep in the same position as ㊾.
Stance: Hachijidachi.
Hands: Stretch the arms up with the backs of both hands facing inward.

●挙動の分解　Kumite in detail

相手が後ろから羽交い絞めに攻めてくる。

Your opponent will pinion you from behind.

両手を上に高く上げる。直ちに腰を落として両肘を強く下に当てるようにして、両肘を自分の腹部の前で強く締めるようにして相手の手を外す。

Raise both hands high. Quickly lower your waist, forcefully thrust downward both of your elbows to tighten firmly in front of your abdomen so that you can release your opponent's hands.

両肘を後方から大きく回し、相手の腕を絞るように両肘を強く自分の腹部前で締めてはずす。

Twist both elbows from behind, and tighten and release both elbows in front of your abdomen in order to squeeze and release your opponent's arms.

途中動作	38 挙動	39 挙動

	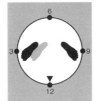	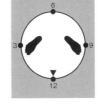
Transition Movement	足の動作／右足を3時方向に移動する。立ち方／四股立ち。手の動作／両肘を下に当てるようにして体の前で締める（手の甲は前に向ける）。 Feet: Bring the right foot in the direction of 3 o'clock. Stance: Shikodachi. Hands: Thrust down both elbows and tight them in front of your body (the back of hand points forward).	足の動作／そのまま。立ち方／四股立ち。手の動作／両腕を後ろに伸ばし、掌底で下方を押さえる。この時、息を吐き、頭部を後方に当てる。 Feet: Keep in the same position as ㊳. Stance: Shikodachi. Hands: Extend both arms to the back, Push downward with Shotei. At this time, Breathe out and hit the head backward.

両手を後ろへ伸ばして相手の両脚を取る。

Extend both hands backward and grab both of your opponent's legs.

後頭部にて相手の顔面に頭突きを行う。この時は口を開いて息を吐く。

Butt the back of your head against your opponent's face. At this time, open your mouth and exhale.

相手の脚を掴んで後ろへ飛び上がるようにして後ろへ倒し、さらに水月に頭突きを行う。

With your opponent's legs seized, jump backwards to throw him down. Butt the back of your head against your opponent's solar plexus.

前に出て伏せ、相手が起き上がる瞬間に後ろ蹴りを行う。

Lie down forward, and do Ushiro-geri at the moment when the opponent gets up.

40 挙動　　41 挙動　　42 挙動

  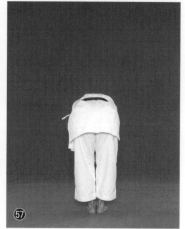

 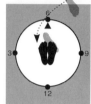  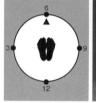 

足の動作／右足を12時方向に移動する。
立ち方／右前屈立ち。
手の動作／開手上段交差受け。

Feet: Bring the right foot in the direction of 12 o'clock.
Stance: Right Zenkutsudachi.
Hands: Do Kaishu Jodan Kousa-uke.

足の動作／左足を右足に引き付け、反時計回りで6時方向を向く。
立ち方／閉足立ち。
手の動作／そのまま。

Feet: Bring the left foot to the right foot. Turn the body counterclockwise in the direction of 6 o'clock.
Stance: Heisokudachi.
Hands: Keep in the same position as ㊾.

足の動作／そのまま。
立ち方／閉足立ち。
手の動作／両手を交差したまま握り、振り下ろして、上体は前へ倒す。

Feet: Keep in the same position as ㊿.
Stance: Heisokudachi.
Hands: With the arms still crossed, and make the hands into fists. While bending the upper body forward, swing down the fists downward.

●挙動の分解　Kumite in detail

相手の上段突きに対し、左足を一歩引き、開手交差受けを行う。ただちに相手の手首を捕る。
Block your opponent's Jodan Zuki by taking a step backward with your left foot and performing a Kaishu Kousa-uke. Quickly seize your opponent's wrist.

右拳にて相手の人中に裏打ちを行う。
Perform an Ura-uchi strike with your right fist against your opponent's philtrum.

両手で相手の手首を取り、下から回すように上に振りかぶる。
Seize your opponent's wrist with both hands and raise your arms to twist it from below.

下に向かって切り下すようにして投げる。
Throw your opponent downward.

43 挙動

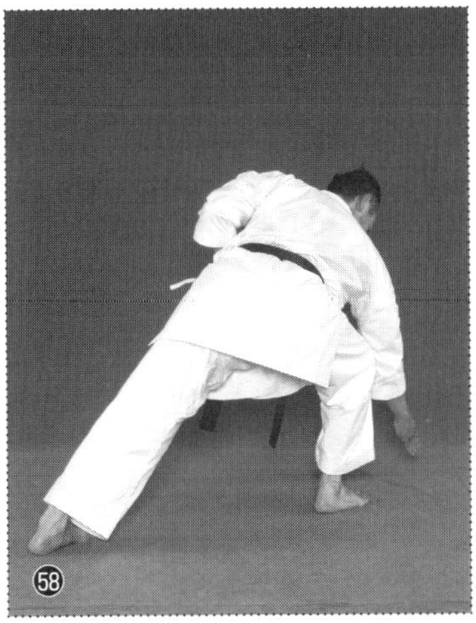

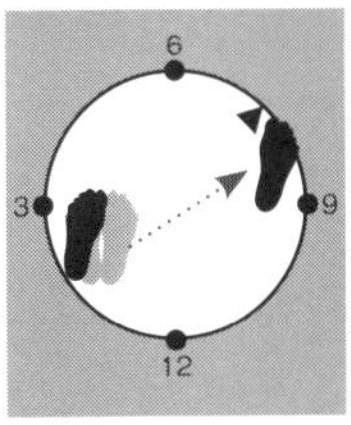

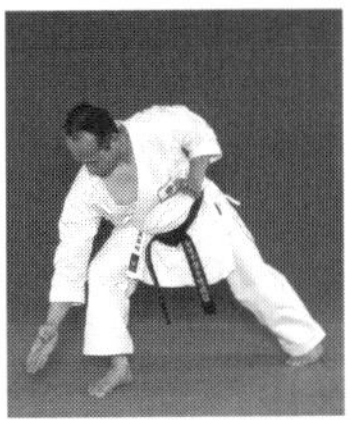

足の動作／右足を右斜め方向へ運び、体は前方へ倒す。目付は、斜め下。
立ち方／深い右前屈立ち。
手の動作／右開手は下方へ伸ばし、左開手は左脇へ構える。

Feet: Bring the right foot diagonally to the right and let the body lean forward. Look obliquely downward.
Stance: Deep Right Zenkutsudachi.
Hands: Stretch the right hand downwards and hold the left hand to the left side.

44 挙動

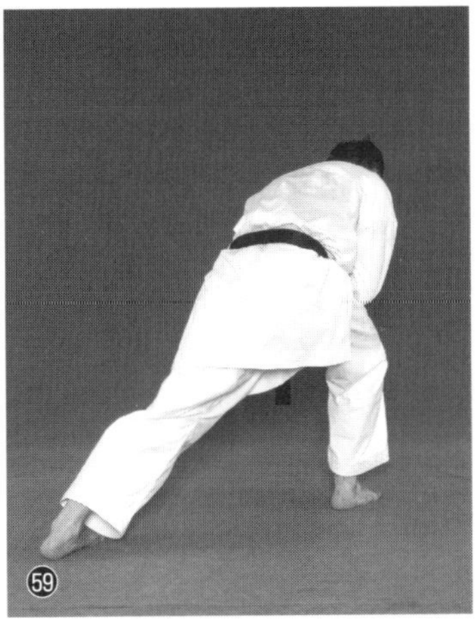

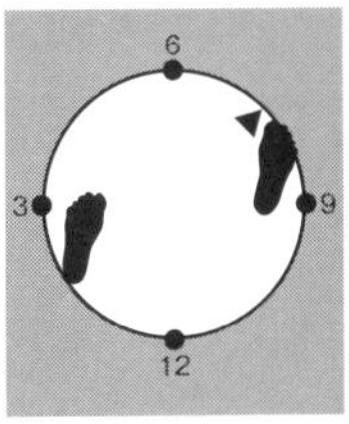

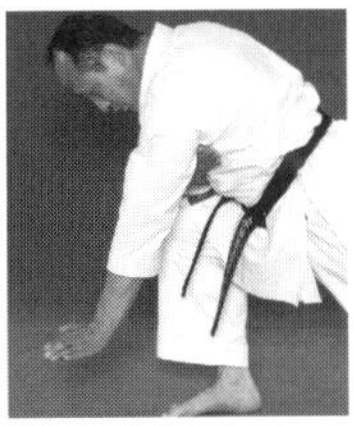

足の動作／そのまま。
立ち方／深い右前屈立ち。
手の動作／左掌底で斜め下方を当て、右手は掌を手前に左脇の下へ引く。

Feet: Keep in the same position as (58) .
Stance: Deep Zenkutsudachi.
Hands: Hit diagonally downward with Left Shote, and pull the right hand with the palm inside to the left armpit.

45 挙動

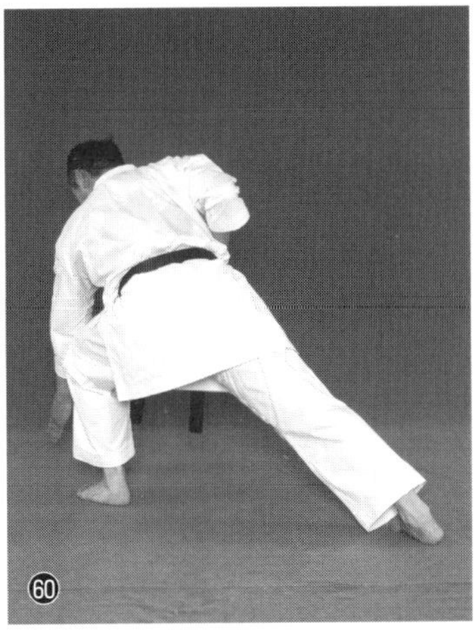

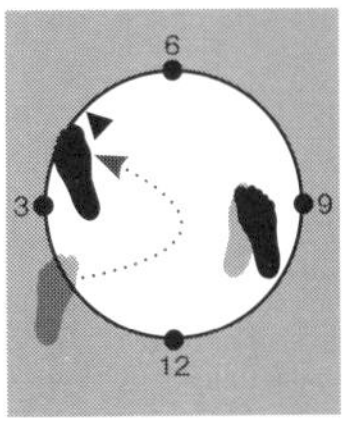

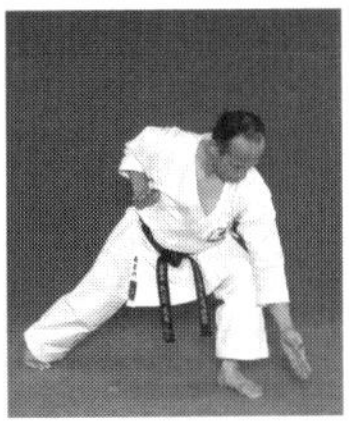

足の動作／左足を左斜め方向へ運び、体は前方へ倒す。目付は、斜め下。
立ち方／深い左前屈立ち。
手の動作／左開手は下方へ伸ばし、右開手は右脇へ構える。

Feet: Bring the left foot diagonally to the left and let the body lean forward.Look obliquely downward.
Stance: Deep Left Zenkutsudachi.
Hands: Stretch the left hand downwards and hold the right hand to the right side.

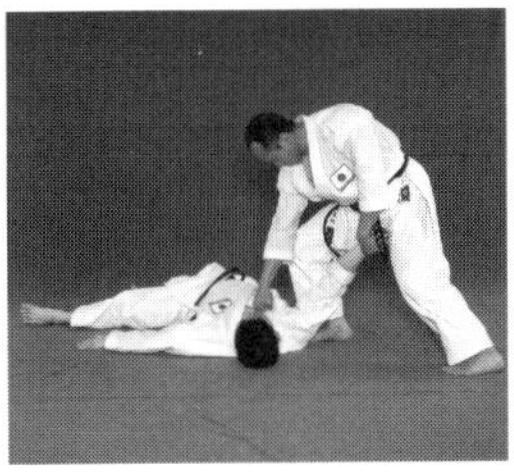

腰を落として突きを極める。

Lower your hips and finish with a Tsuki (punch.)

46 挙動   47 挙動   途中動作

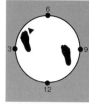

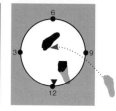
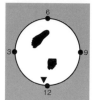

足の動作／そのまま。
立ち方／深い左前屈立ち。
手の動作／右掌底で斜め下方を当て、左手は掌を手前に右脇の下へ引く。

Feet: Keep in the same position as ⓺⓪.
Stance: Deep Left Zenkutsudachi.
Hands: Hit diagonally downward with Right Shote, and pull the left hand with the palm inside to the right armpit.

足の動作／右足を前方へ運び、正面を向く。
立ち方／左猫足立ち。
手の動作／両手の甲を合わせるように右脇へ構える。

Feet: Bring the right foot forward and turn back in the direction of 12 o'clock.
Stance: Left Nekoashidachi.
Hands: Take the backs of both hands face to face and hold them to the right armpit.

Transition Movement

●挙動の分解   Kumite in detail

相手の右中段突きに対し左後方へ転身して猫足立ちとなり、右回し受けを行う。

Block your opponent's Right Chudan Zuki by shifting to the rear left and performing a Right Mawashi-uke in the Nekoashidachi stance.

相手の右腕を取って、関節を極めて押し出す。

Seize your opponent's right arm, lock the joint of his arm and push him away.

48 挙動　　途中動作　　49 挙動

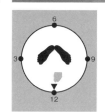
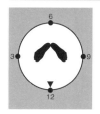

足の動作／そのまま。
立ち方／左猫足立ち。
手の動作／左回し受け。

Feet: Keep in the same position as ㉒.
Stance: Leftt Nekoashidachi.
Hands: Do Left Mawashi-uke.

足の動作／左足を右足の横に引く。
立ち方／結び立ち。
手の動作／両掌を重ね水月前に上げる。

Feet: Pull the left foot to the right foot and take the Musubidachi stance.
Stance: Musubidachi.
Hands: Put both hands together and hold them in front of the solar plexus.

足の動作／そのまま。
立ち方／結び立ち。
手の動作／両掌を重ねて、床を押すように下腹部前に構える。

Feet: Keep in the same position as ㉕.
Stance: Musubidachi.
Hands: Open both hands and hold then in front of the lower abdomen as if pushed down the floor.

クルルンファ

気を付けの姿勢	礼	気を付けの姿勢

足の動作／そのまま。
立ち方／結び立ち。
手の動作／両手を伸ばし、大腿部外側に付ける。

Feet: Keep in the same position as ⑥ .
Stance: Musubidachi
Hands: Stretch both arms with hands putting on both sides of the thighs.

足の動作／そのまま。
立ち方／結び立ち。
手の動作／そのまま。

Feet: Keep in the same position as ⑥ .
Stance: Musubidachi
Hands: Keep in the same position as ⑥ .

足の動作／そのまま。
立ち方／結び立ち。
手の動作／そのまま。

Feet: Keep in the same position as ⑥ .
Stance: Musubidachi
Hands: Keep in the same position as ⑥ .

クルルンファ

STAFF

■監修／Supervisor
岩田　源三
Genzo Iwata

糸東会会長／糸東会本部道場長
昭和33年10月6日生まれ。埼玉県出身。幼少のころから父である岩田万蔵に空手の手ほどきを受ける。
全空連公認7段・教士。
糸東会8段・範士・一級資格審査員。

The President of Shito-kai / The Chief of Shito-kai Head Dojo
Born October 6th, 1958. Raised in Saitama prefecture. Instructed in the basics of karate in childhood by his father, Manzo Iwata.
Japan Karatedo Federation 7th dan certification/kyoshi.
Shito-kai 8th dan/hanshi/1st grade qualification judge.

■監修／Supervisor
野澤　幸洋
Yukihiro Nozawa

糸東会理事長
昭和19年11月20日旧満州国吉林省生まれ。栃木県出身。昭和39年、東洋大学空手道部入部。爾来糸東流岩田万蔵先生に師事。
全空連公認8段・教士。
糸東会8段・範士・1級資格審査員。

The Chairman of Shito-kai
Born November 20th, 1944, in old Manchukuo, Jilin Province. Raised in Tochigi prefecture. In 1964, joined the karate-do club of Toyo University. After that, studied shito-ryu under Manzo Iwata.
Japan Karatedo Federation 8th dan certification/kyoshi.
Shito-kai 8th dan/hanshi/1st grade qualification judge.

■監修／Supervisor
山岡　硯太郎
Kentaro Yamaoka

糸東会技術本部長
昭和21年9月22日生まれ。広島県出身。昭和41年水口博文先生に師事。
全空連公認7段・教士。糸東会8段・範士・1級資格審査員。

The Chief of Shito-kai Technical Division
Born September 22nd, 1946. Raised in Hiroshima prefecture. In 1966, began to study under Hirofumi Mizuguchi.
Japan Karatedo Federation 7th dan certification/kyoshi.
Shito-kai 8th dan/hanshi/1st grade qualification judge.

■演武／Performer
長谷川　克英
Katsuhide Hasegawa

糸東会技術本部選手強化副委員長
昭和40年12月17日生まれ。山梨県出身。県立峡南高等学校空手道部に入部。伊藤柾宏先生に師事。
全空連公認6段・教士・3級資格審査員。
糸東会6段。

The Vice Chairman of Member Strengthening for the Shito-kai Technical Division
Born December 17th, 1965. Raised in Yamanashi prefecture. Joined the Kyonan High School karate-do club. Studied under Masahiro Ito.
Japan Karatedo Federation 6th dan certification/kyoshi/3rd grade qualification judge.
Shito-kai 6th dan.

■演武／Performer
大木　格
Itaru Oki

昭和61年4月16日生まれ。山梨県出身。小学生から空手を始める。樋川光司先生、長谷川伸一先生に師事。
全空連公認5段。
糸東会3段。

Born April 16th, 1986. Raised in Yamanashi prefecture. Started karate in elementary school. Studied under Koji Hikawa and Shinichi Hasegawa.
Japan Karatedo Federation 5th dan certification.
Shito-kai 3rd dan.

■アシスタント／Assistant
木村　治伸
Harunobu Kimura

糸東会技術本部事務長
昭和44年4月14日生まれ。兵庫県出身。昭和63年神戸商船大学空手道部入部。国分和夫先生、久保田徳市先生に師事。
全空連公認6段・錬士・3級資格審査員。
糸東会6段・錬士・3級資格審査員。

The Manager of Shito-kai Technical Division
Born on April 14th, 1969. Raised in Hyogo prefecture. In 1988, joined the karate-do club of Kobe Merchant Marine University. Studied under Kazuo Kokubu and Tokuichi Kubota.
Japan Karatedo Federation 6th dan certification/renshi/3rd grade qualification judge.
Shito-kai 6th dan/renshi/3rd grade qualification judge.

糸東会本部道場　　　　　　　　Shito-kai Head Dojo
糸東会本部事務局　　　　　　　Shito-kai Head Secretariat

〒351-0033　埼玉県朝霞市浜崎 3-8-11　　3-8-11 Hamasaki, Asaka city,
TEL: 048-476-3818　　　　　　　　　　　Saitama prefecture, Japan 351-0033
FAX: 048-476-3869　　　　　　　　　　　TEL:+81-48-476-3818
　　　　　　　　　　　　　　　　　　　FAX:+81-48-476-3869

■ URL
　　http://www.karatedo.co.jp/shitokai/
■ e-mail
　　shitokai@karatedo.co.jp

糸東流空手形全集　　第四巻

平成 30 年 12 月 25 日　第 1 版 1 刷発行

監修　全日本空手道連盟 糸東会
発行　株式会社チャンプ

◆発行／発売
株式会社チャンプ
〒166-0003　東京都杉並区高円寺南 4-19-3
総和第二ビル 2 階
TEL: 03-3315-3190　FAX: 03-3312-8207

◆ SELL
CHAMP Co., Ltd.
2F Sowa 2nd Bld.,
4-19-3 Koenji-minami, Suginami-ku, Tokyo, 166-0003 Japan
TEL:+81-3-3315-3190　FAX:+81-3-3312-8207

URL http://www.karatedo.co.jp/champ/
e-mail:champ@karatedo.co.jp

乱丁・落丁などがありましたらお取り替えします。　　　　　　　　ISBN 978-4-86344-022-7

160